In accordance with the latest syllabus prescribed by the council for the Indian Certificate of Secondary Education Examination, New Delhi.

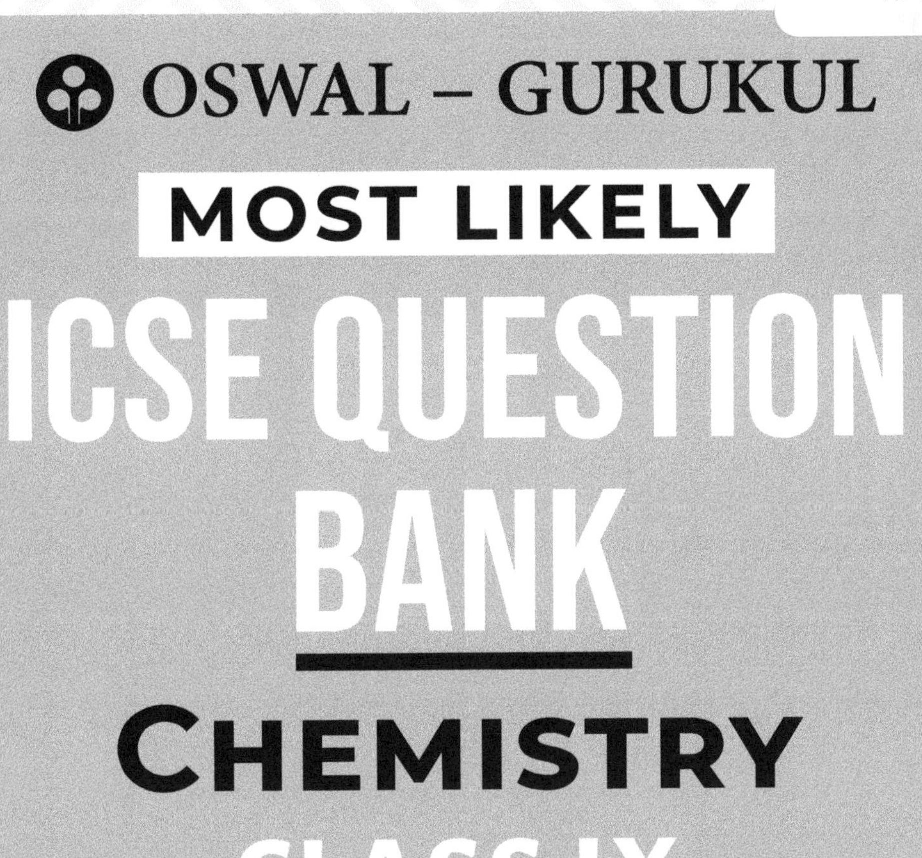

By

PANEL OF AUTHORS

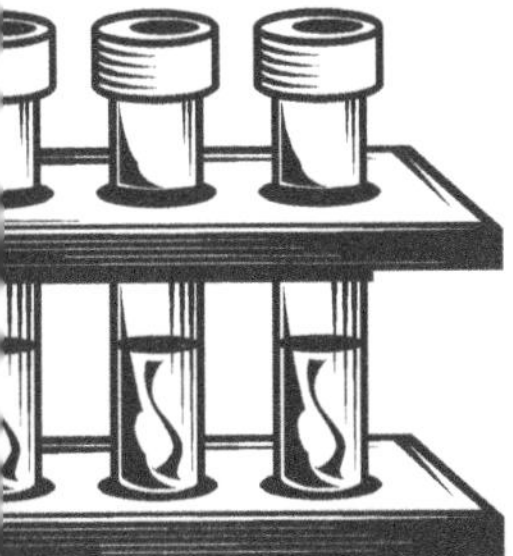

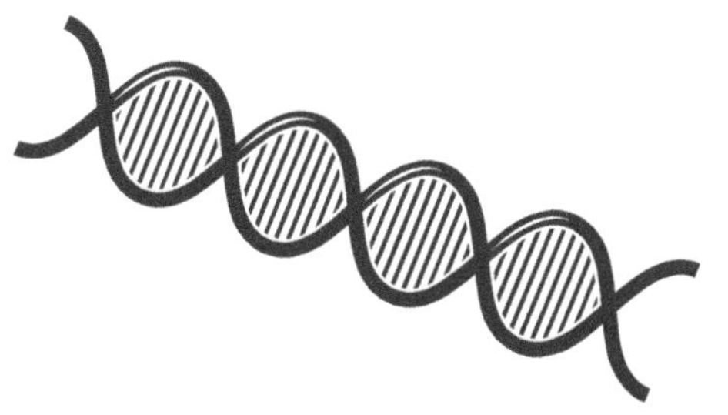

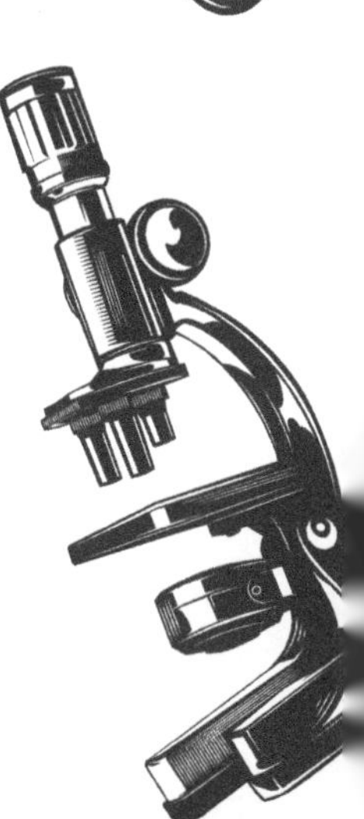

EDITION : 2022

ISBN : 978-93-92563-88-1

PRICE : ₹ 280.00

PRINTED AT :

PUBLISHED BY

OSWAL PUBLISHERS

Head Office : 1/12, Sahitya Kunj, M.G. Road, Agra - 282 002

Phone : (0562) 2527771-4

Whatsapp : +91 74550 77222

E-mail : info@oswalpublishers.in

Website : www.oswalpublishers.com

The cover of this book has been designed using resources from Freepik.com

PREFACE

It is a matter of immense pride for us to present the 'ICSE MOST LIKELY QUESTION BANK' series, especially prepared for students appearing for Board examinations in the oncoming year.

This book has been created with the specific purpose of making the students' journey of learning, understanding and revising the concepts, effortless and simple. The topical approach with ample questions for every category is adopted to reinforce the students' understanding of each chapter. The category-wise division also allows them to peruse their progress as well as keep a check on their grasp of the theory.

Meticulous care has been taken in writing the book in simple, student-friendly language without compromising with the clarity of style.

We are confident that the book will enable the candidates to develop a better understanding of the curriculum and help them organize their learning process. This book shall definitely prove to be a fruitful tool for the students and encourage them towards scholastic excellence.

Constructive suggestions for further improvement of the book are always welcome.

—Publisher

IMPORTANT NOTE

The global outbreak of the Novel Coronavirus (COVID-19) has impacted all aspects of life including the educational life at schools. Schools across the country have been shut since March, 2020 due to the pandemic. While numbers of CISCE affiliated schools have tried to adapt to this changed scenario and have tried to keep alive the teaching learning process through online classes, there has been a significant shortening of the academic year and loss of the instructional hours.

To make up for the loss in instructional hours during the current session 2020-2021, the CISCE has worked with its subject experts, to reduce the syllabi for all major subjects at the ICSE and ISC levels. Syllabus reduction has been done, keeping in mind the linear progression across classes while ensuring that the core concepts related to the subject are retained.

The following reduced syllabi, for the current Academic Year 2020-2021 have been made available on the CISCE website www.cisce.org under 'Publications':

- ICSE Reduced Syllabus for Class IX
- ICSE Reduced Syllabus for Class X
- ISC Reduced Syllabus for Class XI
- ISC Reduced Syllabus for Class XII

Heads of CISCE affiliated schools have been asked to ensure that the concerned subject teachers at the ICSE and ISC levels transact the syllabus strictly according to sequence of topics, so as to facilitate further reduction in syllabus, if required, depending on the situation of the pandemic in the country.

We at Oswal Publishers, have developed all our books on the basis of the original syllabi with complete subjective knowledge of all the subjects, so that the students have an access to the entire syllabus. However, for the examination purpose, the students are advised to structure their preparations considering the latest alterations by the Council.

Scan this to know the recent changes in Syllabus

CONTENTS

How to choose a GREAT CAREER

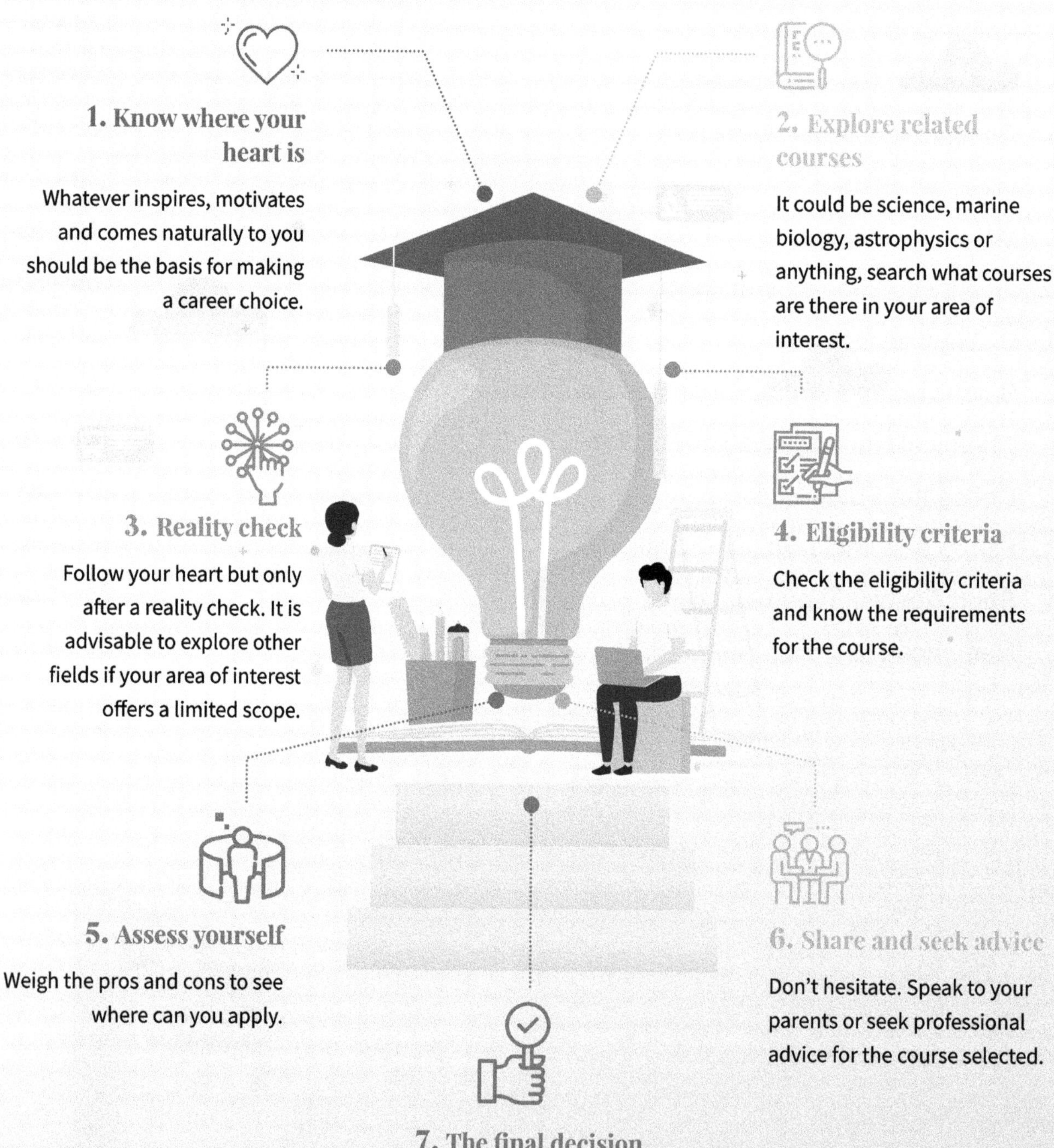

1. Know where your heart is

Whatever inspires, motivates and comes naturally to you should be the basis for making a career choice.

2. Explore related courses

It could be science, marine biology, astrophysics or anything, search what courses are there in your area of interest.

3. Reality check

Follow your heart but only after a reality check. It is advisable to explore other fields if your area of interest offers a limited scope.

4. Eligibility criteria

Check the eligibility criteria and know the requirements for the course.

5. Assess yourself

Weigh the pros and cons to see where can you apply.

6. Share and seek advice

Don't hesitate. Speak to your parents or seek professional advice for the course selected.

7. The final decision

Once you are through with all the steps, you will know where you stand and will be better placed to make the right choice.

Go where your strength is, not where your friends are.

HOW TO MANAGE YOUR TIME BETTER

This is the time when you are going to be promoted to higher classes. Going a level up also means there will be more books, more syllabus, more tests & exams. We have pieced together some of the most effective tips that will surely help you stay ahead of your peers by staying organised and managing your time as well as energy in an improved manner.

- **Make a list:** Every morning, jot down all the things you have to do for the day. Arrange all your tasks according to their importance and urgency. Then, before going to bed, strike off the tasks you managed to finish, giving yourself a sense of accomplishment and helping you stay on track.
- **Segregate your time:** You should divide your day into hourly-chunks, based on your routine. For example, separate about 6-7 compulsory hours for school; then, 7-8 hours for sleep, 4-5 hours for self-study, 1 hour each for leisure and meals. You can keep the remaining hours free as they get used up in chores and other mundane tasks.
- **Improve your focus:** You must strive to finish your tasks in a decided time limit. Learn to eliminate distractions. You should give your undivided attention to their completion. This will improve your efficiency and help you finish your work on time.
- **Take little breaks:** In your study schedule, make sure to assign small breaks between long study sessions to give your brain some rest and restore your energy for another round of rigorous learning. You can have a snack or simply close your eyes and quietly meditate.
- **End procrastination:** Procrastination is the biggest hurdle in your path to success. If you have a daunting task at hand, it's better to break it into smaller chunks and work on them than just postponing it for later. Slow and steady wins the race, after all!

Follow these tips and watch your productivity increase with time. Share your experience with us at contact@oswalpublishers.com .

WEEKLY SCHEDULE

	MONDAY	TUESDAY	WEDNESDAY	THURSDAY	FRIDAY	SATURDAY	SUNDAY

GOALS

DON'T FORGET!

NOTES

Multiple Choice Questions | Set 1 |

Choose the most appropriate answer for each of the following:

Chapter 1. The Language of Chemistry

1. What is the formula of cuprous oxide?
(A) CuO
(B) Cu_2O_2
(C) Cu_2O_2
(D) Cu_3O

2. Which of the following is correct option for a balanced chemical reaction?
(A) $Mg + 2HCl \rightarrow MgCl_2 + H_2$
(B) $NaOH + H_2SO_4 \rightarrow Na_2SO_4 + 2H_2O$
(C) $KNO_3 \rightarrow KNO_2 + O_2$
(D) None of these

3. $Cl_2 +$ .... $+ 2H_2O \longrightarrow H_2SO_4 + 2HCl$ is a balanced chemical equation. Choose the correct option.
(A) SO_3
(B) SO_2
(C) H_2S
(D) $2SO_3$

4. Identify the monovalent cation.
(A) Sodium
(B) Aluminium
(C) Chlorine
(D) None of these

5. What is the empirical formula mass of NH_3?
(A) 17
(B) 20
(C) 15
(D) 18

6. Which of the following represents the formula of a compound?
(A) An atom
(B) A molecule
(C) A combination
(D) All of these

7. What is the valency of nitrogen in the molecule NO_2?
(A) 1
(B) 2
(C) 3
(D) 4

8. How many carbon atoms are present in acetate radical?
(A) One
(B) Two
(C) Three
(D) Four

9. Which of the following is the mass ratio of hydrogen to oxygen?
(A) 1 : 8
(B) 1 : 16
(C) 1 : 32
(D) 1 : 64

10. Identify the formula of calcium hydrogen carbonate if formula of sodium carbonate is Na_2CO_3.
(A) $NaCO_3$
(B) $Ca_2(HCO_3)_2$
(C) Ca_2HCO_3
(D) $Ca\ (HCO_3)_3$

11. The valency of Sulphur in SO_3 is: **[November, 2019]**
(A) Two
(B) Three
(B) Four
(D) Six

12. MOH is the formula of the hydroxide of a metal M. The formula of its sulphate is: **[November, 2019]**
(A) MSO_4
(B) $M(SO_4)_2$
(C) M_2SO_4
(D) $M_2(SO_4)_3$

Ans.

1. (C)	2. (A)	3. (B)	4. (A)
5. (A)	6. (B)	7. (D)	8. (B)
9. (A)	10. (B)	11. (D)	12. (C).

Chapter 2. Chemical Changes and Reactions

1. Identify the incorrect characteristic of chemical change.
   (A) New substance formed (B) Easily reversible
   (C) Involves absorption or liberation of energy (D) None of these
2. Respiration is an example of what type of reaction?
   (A) Endothermic reaction (B) Exothermic reaction
   (C) Both (A) and (B) (D) None of these
3. Identify the substance that undergoes combustion readily and gives energy.
   (A) Carbon dioxide (B) Quicklime
   (C) Methane (D) None of these
4. Name the acid that is released when a bee stung our body.
   (A) Acetic acid (B) Hydrochloric acid
   (C) Ammonia (D) Formic acid
5. Identify the least reactive element.
   (A) Fluorine (B) Iodine
   (C) Chlorine (D) Bromine
6. Which of the following is correct regarding the given chemical reaction?
   $$AB + CD \rightarrow AD + CD$$
   (A) No chemical change occurs (B) Decomposition of AB and CD takes place
   (C) Exchange of ions of AB and CD (D) Combination of AB and CD
7. Identify the product of thermal decomposition of calcium carbonate.
   (A) Carbon dioxide (B) Oxygen
   (C) Calcium hydroxide (D) None of these
8. Chemical change sometimes evolve energy in the form of:
   (A) heat (B) light
   (C) sound (D) All of these
9. When someone is stung by bee, which of the following acid is released by the bee?
   (A) Acetic acid (B) Formic acid
   (C) Lactic acid (D) Hydrochloric acid
10. $BaCl_2(aq) + H_2SO_4(aq) \rightarrow BaSO_4(aq) + 2HCl(aq)$
    Identify the type of reaction.
    (A) Decomposition reaction (B) Neutralisation reaction
    (C) Double decomposition reaction (D) Displacement reaction
11. In which of the following process new substances(s) are formed?
    (A) Melting of ice (B) Sublimation of naphthalene
    (C) Photosynthesis (D) All of these
12. The catalyst used as a promotor for the formation of ammonia gas is:
    (A) Fe (B) Mo
    (C) Pd (D) Ni

13. When crystals of lead nitrate are heated strongly in a dry test tube:
(A) crystals immediately melt
(B) a brown residue is left
(C) white fumes appear in the tube
(D) a yellow residue is left

14. The salt that undergoes photochemical decomposition is: **[February, 2020]**
(A) Copper sulphate
(B) Zinc carbonate
(C) Lead bromide
(D) Silver nitrate

15. Dilute hydrochloric acid is added to granulated zinc taken in a test tube. The following obervations are recorded. Point out the correct observation.
(A) The surface of metal becomes shining
(B) The reaction mixture turns milky
(C) Odour of a pungent smelling gas is recorded
(D) A colourless and odourless gas is evolved

16. On immersing an iron nail in $CuSO_4$ solution for few minutes, you will observe that:
(A) no reaction takes place
(B) the colour of solution fades away
(C) the surface of iron nails acquire a black coating
(D) the colour of solution changes to green

Ans. **1.** (B) **2.** (B) **3.** (C) **4.** (D) **5.** (B) **6.** (C)
7. (A) **8.** (D) **9.** (B) 10. (C) 11. (C) 12. (B)
13. (D) 14. (D) 15. (D) 16. (B)

Chapter 3. Water

1. How much percentage of water on earth is freshwater?
(A) 1%
(B) 2%
(C) 2.5%
(D) 10%

2. How many physical states of water exist?
(A) 2
(B) 3
(C) 1
(D) 4

3. Identify the chemical formula of Glauber's salt.
(A) $Na_2SO_4 . 10H_2O$
(B) $Na_2SO_4.2H_2O$
(C) $Na_2SO_4.2H_2O$
(D) $Na_2SO_4.H_2O$

4. Which of the following is used in drying of gases?
(A) Conc. HNO_3
(B) Conc. H_2SO_4
(C) Conc. HCl
(D) None of the these

5. With the rise in temperature the solubility of sodium chloride in water: **[February, 2020]**
(A) Decreases
(B) Increases and then decreases
(C) Increases sharply
(D) Increases only a little

6. A substance that does not contain water of crystallization is: **[February, 2020]**
(A) Blue vitriol
(B) Common salt
(C) Glauber's salt
(D) Washing soda crystals

7. Which of the following water does not contain dissolved solids?
(A) Tap water
(B) Well water
(C) Rain water
(D) River water

8. Which of the following is not a characteristic of a true solution?
(A) It scatter light
(B) The size of the solute particles are very small
(C) It is clear and transparent
(D) It does not scatter light

9. Alumina is an example of:
(A) Hygroscopic substance
(B) Efflorescence
(C) Drying agent
(D) Dehydrating agent

10. Which one is the chemical formula of Epsom salt?
(A) $MgSO_4.7H_2O$ (B) $MgSO_4.8H_2O$
(C) $MgSO_4.10H_2O$ (D) $MgSO_4.9H_2O$

11. Ferric chloride is a:
(A) Deliquescent salt (B) Efflorescent salt
(C) Hygroscopic in nature (D) None of these

Ans. 1. (C) 2. (B) 3. (C) 4. (B) 5. (D) 6. (B) 7. (C)
8. (A) 9. (D) 10. (A) 11. (A).

Chapter 4. Atomic Structure and Chemical Bonding

1. Which of the following subatomic particle is discovered by E. Goldstein?
(A) Electron (B) Proton
(C) Neutron (D) None of these

2. Identify the isotope which is used for determining the age of historical and geological material.
(A) $^{12}_{6}C$ (B) $^{10}_{6}C$
(C) $^{14}_{6}C$ (D) $^{9}_{6}C$

3. Identify the gas which is not a noble gas.
(A) Argon (B) Helium
(C) Carbon dioxide (D) Neon

4. Which of the following is correct statement regarding metal atoms?
(A) They gain electrons and get oxidised. (B) They gain electrons and get reduced.
(C) They loss electrons and get oxidised. (D) They loss electrons and get reduced.

5. Identify the incorrect statements about isotopes.
(A) They have different mass numbers. (B) They are atoms of same element.
(C) They have same physical properties. (D) They have same chemical properties.

6. Which of the following is discovered in Rutherford's alpha scattering experiment?
(A) Electron (B) Proton
(C) Neutron (D) Nucleus

7. The number of valence electrons in O^{2-} ion are:
(A) 4 (B) 8
(C) 6 (D) 10

8. Identify the correct electronic configuration of potassium.
(A) 2, 8 (B) 2, 8, 9
(C) 2, 8, 1 (D) 2, 8, 5

9. The mass number of an atom whose ion have 10 electrons and 12 neutrons is:
(A) 23 (B) 22
(C) 20 (D) 21

10. How many electrons do the outermost shell of an atom accommodate?
(A) 8 (B) 2
(C) 10 (D) 18

11. J. J. Thomson, in his atomic model, assigned positive charge to:
(A) Electron (B) Proton
(C) Neutron (D) Atomic sphere

12. Which scientist proposed that electrons revolve in distinct energy level around nucleus?
(A) Rutherford (B) Bohr
(C) Chadwick (D) Thomson

13. Isotopes of an element have:
(A) same physical properties (B) diffemt chemical properties
(C) different number of neutrons (D) different atomic numbers

14. Which of the following is a covalent compound? **[February, 2020]**
(A) Sodium chloride (B) Carbon tetrachloride
(C) Magnesium chloride (D) Calcium chloride

15. An element with the atomic number 19 will most likely combine chemically with the element whose atomic number is:
(A) 17 (B) 11
(C) 18 (D) 20

16. The bond formed between nitrogen atoms in a molecule is:
(A) Single covalent bond (B) Double covalent bond
(C) Ionic bond (D) Triple covalent bond

Ans. **1.** (B) **2.** (C) **3.** (C) **4.** (C) **5.** (C) **6.** (D) **7.** (B) **8.** (C) **9.** (A) **10.** (A) **11.** (D) **12.** (B) **13.** (C) **14.** (B) **15.** (A) **16.** (D).

Chapter 5. The Periodic Table

1. Which type of elements are shown in bottom of periodic table?
(A) Noble gas (B) Inner transition elements
(C) Transition elements (D) Representative elements

2. Identify the typical element from the following.
(A) Mg (B) Na
(C) Si (D) All of these

3. Down the group metallic character:
(A) increases (B) decreases
(C) increases up to some element and then decrease (D) decrease upto some element and then increase

4. Which of the following is the largest atom?
(A) Oxygen (B) Nitrogen
(C) Fluorine (D) Beryllium

5. What is the physical state of bromine?
(A) Liquid (B) Solid
(C) Gas (D) None of these

6. How many electrons are present in the outermost orbit of alkaline earth metals?
(A) Zero (B) One
(C) Two (D) Three

7. Find the odd one out.
(A) Beryllium (B) Rubidium
(C) Calcium (D) Strontium

8. Which of the element of group 17 is solid in nature?
(A) Chlorine (B) Fluorine
(C) Bromine (D) Iodine

9. Valency of lithium is:
(A) 1 (B) 3
(C) 2 (D) 0

10. Group 18 elements are known as:
(A) Alkaline earth metal (B) Alkali metal
(C) Halogen (D) Noble gas

11. Which of the following is the correct set of elements to Dobereiner's triads?
(A) Li Na K
7 23 39
(B) Br Cl I
80 355 127
(C) Fe Ni Co
55.85 58.71 58.93
(D) Data is insufficient

12. Which of the following statement(s) about the modern periodic table are incorrect?
I. The elements in the modern periodic table are arranged on the basis of their decreasing atomic number.
II. The elements in the modern periodic table are arranged on the basis of their increasing atomic masses.
III. Isotopes are placed in adjoining group (s) in the periodic table.
IV. The elements in the modern periodic table are arranged on the basis of their increasing atomic number.
(A) Only I (B) I, II, and III
(C) I, II and IV (D) Only IV

Ans. 1. (B) 2. (D) 3. (A) 4. (C) 5. (A) 6. (C) 7. (B)
8. (D) 9. (A) 10. (D) 11. (A) 12. (B)

Chapter 6. Hydrogen

1. Identify the least reactive metal from the following.
(A) Zn (B) Au
(C) Hg (D) H

2. Which metal cannot displace hydrogen from dilute acid?
(A) Copper (B) Mercury
(C) Gold (D) All of these

3. Which of the following statement is/are correct regarding hydrogen?
(A) It is very light gas (B) It is a strong oxidising agent
(C) It has valency two (D) All are correct

4. On reaction of an active metal with water:
(A) Base is produced (B) Carbon dioxide gas is produced
(C) Acid is produced (D) Both (A) and (B)

5. Which of the following does not give hydrogen on reacting with dilute HCl?
(A) Copper (B) Zinc
(C) Iron (D) Magnesium

6. What is the valency of hydrogen?
(A) Zero (B) One
(C) Two (D) Three

7. Potassium is kept in kerosene oil because:
(A) It is soluble in kerosene (B) It catches fire in air
(C) Both (A) and (B) (D) None of these

8. Magnesium burns in steam with an:
   (A) intense white light (B) pale white light
   (C) intense yellow light (D) intense blue light
9. Calcium is not used in laboratory preparation of hydrogen because:
   (A) It reacts violently with acid (B) It forms a protective coating
   (C) It is very expensive (D) All of these
10. Which metal given hydrogen on reacting with water, acid and alkali? **[February, 2020]**
   (A) Iron (B) Zinc
   (C) Magnesium (D) Lead
11. Carbon dioxide, in Bosch process is separated as:
   (A) $CaCO_3$ (B) $NaHCO_3$
   (C) Na_2CO_3 (D) H_2CO_3
12. Hydrogen is collected through:
   (A) air displacement method (B) water displacement method
   (C) Both (a) and (b) (D) Neither (a) nor (b)
13. Solubility of hydrogen in water is:
   (A) very low (B) moderate
   (C) high (D) cannot be determined
14. Zinc metal reacts with sulphuric acid:
   (A) explosively (B) fast
   (C) slowly (D) does not react
15. The catalyst used during Haber's process is:
   (A) Platinum (B) Zinc
   (C) Iron (D) Copper
16. The promoter used during Haber's process is:
   (A) Molybdenum (B) Copper
   (C) Zinc (D) Lead
17. The metal which does not displace hydrogen from dilute acid is:
   (A) soldium (B) copper
   (C) zinc (D) iron
18. On addition of hydrogen ethene gets converted to:
   (A) ethyne (B) methane
   (C) propane (D) ehtane
19. On adding water to sodium the solution formed is:
   (A) neutral (B) alkaline
   (C) acidic (D) amphoteric
20. The gas which has a rotten egg smell is: **[November, 2019]**
   (A) Hydrogen Sulphide (B) Ammonia
   (C) Sulphur dioxide (D) Nitrogen dioxide
21. Which of the following properities ofor hydrogen is true? **[November, 2019]**
   (A) It does not combine with halogen (B) Its combustion is not exothermic
   (C) It is a monoatomic element (D) It is the lightest element.
22. Which of the stastement about the reaction below is incorrect?
   $2PbO(s) + C(s) \rightarrow 2Pb(s) + CO_2(g)$
   (A) Lead is getting reduced (B) Carbon is getting oxidised
   (C) Lead oxide is getting reduced (D) Cannot be predicted

Ans. 1. (B) 2. (D) 3. (A) 4. (C) 5. (A) 6. (B) 7. (B)
8. (A) 9. (C) 10. (C) 11. (D) 12. (B) 13. (A) 14. (C)
15. (C) 16. (A) 17. (B) 18. (D) 19. (B) 20. (A) 21. (D)
22. (A)

Chapter 7. Study of Gas Laws

1. Which of the following is the unit of volume?
   (A) cm^2 (B) cm^3
   (C) cm (D) None of these
2. 1 atm is equal to:
   (A) 700 torr (B) 600 torr
   (C) 760 torr (D) 400 torr
3. At high altitudes, atomospheric pressure is:
   (A) High (B) Low
   (C) Very high (D) Absent
4. Volume-temperature relationship is given by:
   (A) Charles (B) Boyle
   (C) Gay-Lussac (D) Henry
5. The melting point of ice is:
   (A) 0 K (B) 273 K
   (C) – 273 K (D) 100 K
6. What is the ice point in absolute temperature?
   (A) 0 K (B) 273 K
   (C) 215 K (D) – 273 K
7. S.I. unit of pressure, variable of gas law is:
   (A) Kelvin (B) Cubic meter
   (C) Pascal (D) Cubic centimeter
8. How does the temperature relate to kinetic energy of molecules?
   (A) Kinetic energy of the molecule is directly proportional to the temperature.
   (B) Kinetic energy of the molecule is inversely proportional to the temperature.
   (C) There is no relation between temperature and kinetic energy of the molecules.
   (D) None of these
9. If pressure is doubled for a fixed mass of gas, volume will become:
   (A) 2 times (B) 1/2 times
   (C) 4 times (D) No change
10. The absolute temperature value that corresponds to 28°C is:
   (A) 28 K (B) 287 K
   (C) 301 K (D) 273 K
11. The first reliable measurement on the properites of gases was made by scientist............
   (A) Dalton (B) Robert Brown
   (C) Robert Boyle (D) Jacques Charles'
12. The pressure exerted by the gas is due to:
   (A) the repulsion between gas molecules (B) the attraction between gas molecules
   (C) collision of the particles with the wall of the container (D) Both (A) and (B)

Multiple Choice Questions

13. Which of the expression represent the Bolye's law?

(A) $p \propto \frac{1}{V}$ (at constant T and n)

(B) $p \propto \frac{1}{T}$ (at constant V and n)

(C) p ∝ V (at constant T and n)

(D) All of these

14. Boyle's is valid for:

(i) pV = constnt

(ii) $\frac{p_1}{V_2} = \frac{p_2}{V_1}$

(ii)

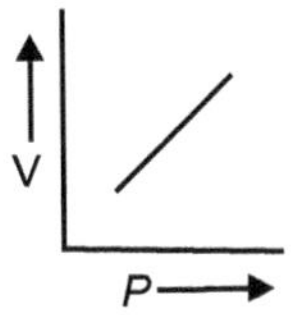

Which of the following is the correct option?

(A) (i) and (iii)

(B) (i) and (ii)

(C) (ii) and (iii)

(D) (i), (ii) and (iii)

15. Charles' law is represented mathematically as:

(A) pV = constant

(B) $V_t = V_0\left(1+\frac{273}{t}\right)$

(C) $V_t = \left(1+\frac{t}{273}\right)$

(D) $\frac{V_t}{V_0} = \frac{T_0}{T_t}$

16. What will be the minimum pressure required compress 2 L of gas at 1 bar to 1 L at 25°C?

(A) 1 bar

(B) 2 bar

(C) 4 bar

(D) 6 bar

17. Point out the correct relationship regarding ideal gas law:

(A) $\frac{pV}{T}$ = constant

(B) $\frac{p_1V_1}{T_1} = \frac{p_2V_2}{T_2}$

(C) Both (A) and (B)

(D) None of these

18. Which of the following options represent an ideal gas equation?

(A) $pV = RT$

(B) $p = VRT$

(C) $pRT = V$

(D) $pVT = R$

19. "At constant temperature, the pressure of a fixed amount of gas varies inversely with its volume". This is known as.........A............Here, A refers to :

(A) Charles' law

(B) Boyle's law

(C) Newton's law

(D) Dalton's law

20. The absolute temperature that corresponds to 26°C is: **[November, 2019]**

(A) 247 K

(B) 226 K

(C) 299 K

(D) 326 K

21. At S.T.P., what is the weight of 22.4 litres of NH_3?

(A) 15 g

(B) 17 g

(C) 22.5 g

(D) 20 g

22. Which of the following is standard pressure?

(A) 700 mm Hg

(B) 560 mm Hg

(C) 760 min Hg

(D) 600 mm Hg

23. Solubility of gases in liquid depends on:
(A) Temperature (B) Pressure
(C) Both A and B (D) None of these

24. The effect of temperature on the solubility of gas in a liquid is governed by:
(A) Boyle's Law (B) Charle's Law
(C) Henry's Law (D) Avogadro's Law

Ans.

1. (B)	2. (C)	3. (B)	4. (C)	5. (B)	6. (C)	7. (C)
8. (A)	9. (B)	10. (D)	11. (C)	12. (C)	13. (A)	14. (B)
15. (C)	16. (B)	17. (C)	18. (A)	19. (B)	20. (C)	21. (B)
22. (C)	23. (B)	24. (C)				

Chapter 8. Atmospheric Pollution

1. Which of the following is the cause of asthma?
(A) Tobacco (B) Cotton dust
(C) Lead (D) Carbon dioxide

2. Which one of the following is not an inert gas?
(A) Oxygen (B) Carbon dioxide
(C) Methane (D) Helium

3. Which one of the following gas is produced by metallurgical process involving sulphide ore?
(A) H_2S (B) SO_2
(C) H_2SO_4 (D) $CaSO_4$

4. Which one of the following gas can trap heat?
(A) Oxygen (B) Methane
(C) Sulphur (D) Hydrogen

5. What one the following is the cause of skin cancer?
(A) Chloro-fluoro-carbons (B) $CaSO_4$
(C) Ultraviolet rays (D) Nitrogen oxide

6. Identify the pollutant which causes smog.
(A) Oxides of sulphur (B) Oxides of nitrogen
(C) Both (A) and (B) (D) None of these

7. Which of the following is caused when excessive carbon dioxide is released?
(A) Formation of smog (B) Depletion of ozone layer
(C) Global warming (D) None of these

8. Which of the following is not the way to reduce global warming?
(A) Deforestation (B) Minimise use of vehicles
(C) Planting trees (D) None of these

9. Identify the pollutant that affects teeth and bones.
(A) Carbon monoxide (B) Carbon dioxide
(C) Nitrogen oxide (D) Fluoride

10. Which of the following gas is released in forest fires?
(A) Carbon dioxide (B) Carbon monoxide
(C) Hydrogen sulphide (D) All of these

11. The major sources of water vapours are:
(A) industrial and vehicular exhaust (B) burning of fuels
(C) volcanic eruptions (D) All of these

12. Which of the following is not a green house gas?

(A) CO (B) CO_2

(C) CH_4 (D) H_2O/vapour

13. For the preparation of ozone, the common used ozoniser is/are

(A) Siemen's ozoniser (B) Brodie's ozoniser

(C) Both (A) and (B) (D) None of these

14. Consider the following measures regarding way to reduce the presence of greenhouse gases.

I. Afforesation

II. Use of solar energy

III. Pooling of cars can be practised

The correct option is:

(A) Only I (B) Only II

(C) I and III (D) I, II and III

Ans. **1.** (B) **2.** (A) **3.** (B) **4.** (B) **5.** (C) **6.** (C) **7.** (C)

8. (A) **9.** (D) **10.** (B) **11.** (D) **12.** (A) **13.** (C) **14.** (B)

❑

Give One Word

Set 2

Give one word for the following statements:

Chapter 1. Language of Chemistry

1. Combining capacity of an atom or radical.
2. Sum of atomic masses of various elements present in the empirical formula.
3. The symbolic representation of a chemical reaction using the symbols and formulae of the substance involved in the reaction.
4. A short-hand notation for the molecules in terms of symbols.
5. The smallest particle that has the capability to exist independently.
6. An ion composed of more than one element.
7. A formula which gives the simplest ratio in whole number of atoms of different elements in a compound.
8. Law that states that matter is neither created nor destroyed.
9. Elements having three atoms in their molecule.
10. An atom or a group of atoms of the same or of different elements that behaves as a single unit with a positive or negative charge.

Ans. 1. Valency 2. Empirical formula mass 3. Chemical equation
4. Molecular formula 5. Molecule 6. Polyatomic ion
7. Empirical formula 8. Law of conservation of matter 9. Triatomic molecule
10. Radical

Chapter 2. Chemical Changes and Reactions

1. A reaction in which heat is liberated.
2. The decomposition which takes place when electricity is passed.
3. A catalyst that accelerates a reaction.
4. The formation of gas bubbles in a liquid during a reaction.
5. The insoluble substance formed in a chemical reaction.
6. A chemical reaction in which two compounds in their aqueous state react to form an insoluble salt.
7. Substances that influence the rate of a chemical reaction by improving the efficiency of the catalysts.
8. The reaction in which a compound splits into two or more simpler substances.
9. A chemical change in which more active element displaces a less active element from its salt solution.
10. A catalyst that accelerates a reaction.

Ans. 1. Exothermic reaction 2. Electrolytic decomposition 3. Positive catalyst
4. Effervescence 5. Precipitate 6. Precipitation reaction
7. Promoters 8. Decomposition reaction 9. Displacement reaction
10. Positive catalyst

Chapter 3. Water

1. A solvent that has the ability to dissolve a wide range of substance in it.
2. The amount of heat energy required by ice to change into water.

3. A mixture of two or more compounds whose composition may be gradually changed by changing the relative amounts of components.
4. A solution in which size of the solute particles is about 10^{-10} m.
5. A solution that holds more solute than its saturated solution at that temperature.
6. A solution where solvent is a liquid other than water
7. A substance which absorbs moisture from the atomosphere, but does not form solution.
8. The substance that can remove combined elements of water in the ratio of 2 : 1 (hydrogen and oxygen) from a compound.
9. A compound which loses its water of crystallisation on exposure to dry air.
10. A substance which contains water of crystallisation.
11. A salt of calcium that causes temporary hardness of water.
12. A salt of magnesium that causes permanent hardness of water.

Ans. 1. Universal solvent 2. Latent heat of fusion 3. Homogeneous mixture 4. True solution 5. Supersaturated solution 6. Non-aqueous solution 7. Hygroscopic substance 8. Dehydrating agent 9. Efflorescence 10. Hydrated substance 11. $Ca(HCO_3)_2$ 12. $MgCl_2$

Chapter 4. Atomic Structure and Chemical Bonding

1. A subatomic particle of an atom with no charge and mass almost equal to the mass of proton.
2. They are imaginary paths where electrons revolve around the nucleus of the atom.
3. The number of electrons of an atom taking part in the formation of shared pairs.
4. Force of attraction between the two atoms that binds them together as a unit is called molecule.
5. The number of electrons gained, lost or shared to attain octet in the outermost shell, gives the combining capacity of the element.
6. They are elements with five, six or seven electrons in their valence shells.
7. They are atoms of same element differ in physical properties.
8. A charged particle formed due to the gain or loss of one or more electrons by an atom.
9. The bond formed due to electrostatic force of attraction between a cation and an anion.
10. Molecule formed due to sharing of electrons.

Ans. 1. Neutron 2. Orbit 3. Covalency 4. Chemical bond 5. Valency 6. Non metals 7. Isotopes 8. Ion 9. Electrovalent bond 10. Covalent molecule

Chapter 5. The Periodic Table

1. A chart of elements prepared in such a way that elements with similar properties occur in the same vertical column.
2. Atoms of same element having similar chemical properties but different atomic masses.
3. Properties that reappear at regular intervals or in which there is gradual variation.
4. Elements that have two outermost shells incomplete.
5. Elements that react with water to form hydroxides which are strong alkali.
6. Vertical columns in the periodic table.
7. Elements of group IIIB (group number 3) of the seventh period.
8. Number of electrons present in valance shell.
9. Group whose elements have zero valency.
10. The element of lanthanides and actinides collectively known elements.

Ans. 1. Periodic table 2. Isotopes 3. Periodic properties
4. Transition elements 5. Alkali metals 6. Groups
7. Actinides 8. Valency 9. Inert gas
10. Inner transition element

Chapter 6. Hydrogen

1. The process by which an atom gains electrons.
2. Arrangement of metals in decreasing order of reactivity in the form of a series.
3. A reaction in which oxidation and reduction takes place simultaneously.
4. A compound which react with both acids and bases.
5. A substance which transfers oxygen to another substance, or removes hydrogen from that substance.
6. An equilibrium that is attained through a chemical change.
7. The process in which an atom or ion loses electron.
8. A process in which an atom or ion gains electrons.
9. Direct combination of hydrogen with organic compounds containing double or triple bonds.
10. A substance which transfers hydrogen to another substance, or removes oxygen from that substance.

Ans. 1. Reduction 2. Reactivity series of metals 3. Redox reaction
4. Amphoteric compound 5. Oxidising agent 6. Chemical equilibrium
7. Oxidation 8. Reduction 9. Hydrogenation
10. Reducing agent

Chapter 7. Study of Gas Laws

1. The process of gradual mixing of two substances kept in contact by molecular motion.
2. A gas law which states that volume of a given mass of dry gas is inversely proportional to its pressure at constant temperature.
3. The temperature at which molecular motion completely ceases on the Kelvin scale.
4. Laws that describe the behavior of a gas under known conditions of pressure, volume and temperature.
5. The force which a gas exerts in unit cross-sectional area on the walls of its container.

Ans. 1. Diffusion 2. Boyle's law 3. Absolute zero
4. Gas laws 5. Pressure

Chapter 8. Atmospheric Pollution

1. Degradation of air quality due to concentration of harmful contaminants that affects human, plant and animal lives.
2. A pollutant that is a combination of oxides of nitrogen and sulphur; and of partially oxidised hydrocarbons and their derivatives that is produced by industries and automobiles as a dark, thick, dust and soot laden fog.
3. A component that causes destruction of vegetation and affects teeth and bones.
4. Glaciers melt; more water evaporates and pattern of rainfall changes.
5. A light bluish gas is found in the upper layer of atmosphere.
6. Heating of earth and its environment due to solar radiation trapped by carbon dioxide and water vapour in the atmosphere.

7. The effect of undesirable changes in our surroundings that have harmful effects on plants, animals and humna beings.
8. The gases which are responsible for the heating of earth.
9. Locking of chlorine monoxide and free radicals of chlorine.
10. Toxic and harmful substances that have an undesirable impact on different components of the environment and life forms.

Ans. **1.** Air pollution **2.** Smog **3.** Fluorides **4.** Global warming **5.** Ozone **6.** Greenhouse effect **7.** Environment pollution **8.** Greenhouse gas **9.** Scavenging **10.** Pollutants.

❑

Name One for Underlined

Set 3

Name one for the underlined terms in a sentence:

Chapter 1. Language of Chemistry

1. Metals form cation to attain stable configuration.
2. Some elements possesses variable valency.
3. Radical having less electrons than the atom
4. Naming of binary acids is given by adding the prefix 'hydro' and the suffix 'ic' to the name of second element.
5. Non-metals can accept electron.
6. An acid radical having two carbon atoms.
7. A trivalent basic radical that can not lose electrons further.
8. An acidic radical formed by three types of atoms.
9. An element having eight atoms in their molecule.
10. A monoatomic noble gas having zero valency.

Ans. **1.** Sodium **2.** Iron **3.** Na^+

4. HCl (Hydrochloric acid) **5.** Oxygen **6.** Acetate (CH_3COO^-)

7. Al^{3+} **8.** HCO_3^- **9.** Sulphur (S_8)

10. Helium.

Chapter 2. Chemical Change and Reaction

1. The reaction between an acid and base produces salt and water.
2. Promoters improve the efficiency of catalyst.
3. Decomposition of compounds of metals by heat is based on their reactivity.
4. Metal bicarbonate gives metal carbonate, water vapour and carbon dioxide.
5. Catalysts are very useful in chemical reaction.
6. A compound that breaks up that decomposes by absorbing sound energy.
7. A metal carbonate that is soluble in water.
8. A process in our body which is an example of decomposition reaction.
9. A metal carbonate which is stable to heat.
10. A metal hydroxide which is stable to heat.
11. A metal carbonate which does not decompose on heating. **[November, 2019]**
12. A dilute acid which cannot be used for the laboratory preparation of hydrogen. **[November, 2019]**
13. A metal nitrate which produces a brown gas on heating and the residue is yellow when hot, white when cold. **[November, 2019]**

Ans. 1. NaCl 2. Molybdenum 3. Sodium
4. Calcium hydrogen corbonate ($Ca(HCO_3)_2$) 5. MnO_2 6. Acetylene
7. Sodium carbonate 8. Digestion of food 9. Sodium carbonate
10. Potassium hydroxide 11. Sodium carbonate (Na_2CO_3) 12. Nitric acid (HNO_3)
13. Lead nitrate [$Pb(NO_3)_2$].

Chapter 3. Water

1. A homogeneous solution of a solid into another solid is called solid solution.
2. Some substances show considerable increase in their solubility with rise in temperature.
3. Some compounds loses its water of crystallisation on exposure to dry air.
4. Drying agents are the substances that can readily absorb moisture from other substances without chemically reacting with them.
5. Some substance has negligible solubility and they are called insoluble.
6. A crystalline substance which do not contain water of crystallisation.
7. A substance which is used to absorb water vapour from the air.
8. An air tight glass vessel which contains suitable drying agent at the bottom.
9. A mineral which is found in abundance in large deposits of volcano tuff.
10. A solution in which more of the solute can be dissolved at a given temperature.

Ans. 1. Brass 2. Sodium nitrate 3. Glauber's salt
4. Phosphorus pentoxide 5. Silver chloride 6. Common salt (NaCl)
7. Desiccating agent 8. Desiccator 9. Zeolite
10. Unsaturated solution.

Chapter 4. Atomic Structure and Chemical Bonding

1. Inert gases are chemically inactive.
2. Isotopes differ in few physical properties such as density, boiling point, etc.
3. Elements having one, two or three valences are generally metals.
4. Bonds formed between metals and non-metals are ionic or electrovalent bond.
5. An electronegative atom gains electrons and undergoes reduction.
6. Metals can form cation by losing its electrons.
7. Ionic compounds are stable due to electrostatic force of attraction.
8. A covalent compound is formed due to mutual sharing of electrons.
9. An element that has three isotopes.
10. An element which is a good reducing agent.

Ans. 1. Helium 2. Hydrogen (Protium, Deuterium, tritium) 3. Covalency
4. Sodium 5. Fluorine 6. Sodium
7. Sodium chloride 8. Water 9. Carbon
10. Sodium.

Chapter 5. The Periodic Table

1. An alkali metal which is very reactive.
2. Elements of zero group are chemically inactive.

3. A transition element that is used as catalyst.
4. Elements that have two valence electrons.
5. Halogen that is most reactive.
6. The gas which is used in airships.
7. An element whose properties were predicted on the basis of its position in Mendeleev's periodic table.
8. An element of group 18 which can form compounds.
9. An element having 2 electrons in their valenced shell.
10. A metal of group III A.

Ans. 1. Sodium 2. Helium 3. Iron 4. Magnesium 5. Fluorine 6. Helium 7. Eka-silicon 8. Xenon or krypton 9. Magnesium 10. Aluminium.

Chapter 6. Hydrogen

1. Oxide of active metals have great affinity towards oxygen.
2. In the presence of a catalyst hydrogen directly combines with organic compounds.
3. A metal which is below hydrogen in activity series of metals.
4. A metal that displace hydrogen from dilute acid with explosive violence.
5. A gas that can be removed by passing hydrogen through lead nitrate solution.
6. A metal react with steam to form oxides of metals and evolve hydrogen gas.
7. A gas that is strong reducing agent.
8. A metal which is very expensive so that it is not used in laboratory preparation of hydrogen from acid.
9. A non-metal which is a present in activity series of metals.
10. A solution used to remove phosphine from hydrogen.

Ans. 1. Sodium 2. Nickel 3. Copper 4. Sodium 5. Hydrogen sulphide 6. Aluminium 7. Hydrogen 8. Calcium 9. Hydrogen 10. Silver nitrate solution.

Chapter 7. Study of Gas Laws

1. The law according to which at constant pressure, the volume of a given mass of gas is directly proportional to its absolute temperature.
2. The hypothetical temperature at which gases are supposed to occupy zero volume.
3. A hypothetical gas which follow Boyle's law, Charles' law and Avogadro's law in all conditions of temperatures and pressures.
4. A measurement for height of mercury column.
5. The standard temperature which is reference point as STP for general convention.

Ans. 1. Charles law 2. –273.15°C 3. Ideal gas 4. in millimetre (mm Hg) 5. 0°C (273k)

Chapter 8. Atmospheric Pollution

1. A gaseous pollutant that causes lung cancer.
2. A gas that causes irritation in mucous membrane.
3. A poisonous gas with chlorine like smell.
4. A gas that is released by refrigerators and air-conditioning system.
5. The layer acts as a blanket in the atmosphere.
6. An acid responsible for acid rain.
7. A gas that is emitted in large quantities during anaerobic respiration of organic matter in soil, water and sediments.
8. A gas that is found in the upper layer of atomosphere.
9. A chemical that depletes the ozone layer.
10. A compound of oxygen which is produced due to burning of fuels in furnaces.

Ans. **1.** Tobacco smoke **2.** Nitrogen dioxide **3.** Ozone
4. CFC **5.** Ozone layer **6.** Nitric acid
7. Methane **8.** Ozone **9.** Chlorofluorocarbon (CFC)
10. Nitric oxide

❑

Reasoning Based Questions | Set 4 |

Give reason for each of the following:

Chapter 1. Language of Chemistry

1. Some elements exhibit variable valency.
2. C-12 is used as standard unit in measurement of atomic mass of elements.
3. A chemical equation should be balanced.
4. Atomicity of noble gases is one.
5. Basic unit of matter in any state is molecules.
6. Sulphur is an octatomic molecule.
7. The symbol for sodium is 'Na' instead of 'S'.
8. Valency of an element depends upon number of valence electrons.
9. The symbol of copper is 'Cu' not 'Co'.

Ans.

1. An atom of an element can sometimes lose more electrons than those present in its valence shell, *i.e,* there is a loss of electrons from the penultimate shell too. Therefore, such an element is said to exhibit variable valency.
2. In the beginning the mass of hydrogen atom was chosen as a unit and masses of other atoms were compared with it. C-12 was finally selected because its adoption least affected the values of the atomic mass of the various elements on the old standard.
3. An equation must be balanced in order to comply with the "Law of conservation of matter", which states that matter is neither created nor destroyed in the course of a chemical reaction. An unbalanced equation would imply that atoms have been created or destroyed.
4. The number of atoms in a molecule of an element is called its atomicity. Noble gases like helium, neon, argon, krypton, xenon, etc. have one atom each in their molecule. So, atomicity of noble gases is one.
5. The basic unit of matter in any state is molecules because molecule is the smallest particle of matter which has independent existence.
6. Sulphur molecule has eight sulphur atoms. So, it is called as octatomic molecule.
7. The symbol of sodium is taken from its Latin name 'Natrium'. So, its symbol is 'Na'.
8. Valency of an element is the number of electrons that an element can lose or gain. So, valency depends on number of electrons in the valence shell.
9. The symbol of copper is taken from its Latin name that is 'Cuprum'.

Chapter 2. Chemical Change and Reaction

1. Solutions of silver nitrate and hydrogen peroxide are kept in brown bottles.
2. Enzymes are examples of positive catalyst.
3. Promoters play a crucial role in chemical reaction.
4. Blue colour copper sulphate solution turns to light green on addition of few pieces of iron.
5. Slaked lime is used for white washing.
6. Molybdenum is used in manufacture of ammonia.

7. Colourless concentrated sulphuric acid in a test tube changes to blue on adding a small piece of copper to it.
8. When dilute hydrochloric acid is added to calcium carbonate effervescence takes place.
9. Reaction of iron and copper sulphate produces ferrous sulphate and copper.

Ans.

1. Solutions of silver nitrate and hydrogen peroxide are kept in brown bottles in the laboratory because they decompose in the presence of light.
2. Enzymes act as catalyst in biochemical reaction. During digestion, the complex food material breaks down into simpler substances in two to three hours in the presence of enzymes acting as catalyst.
3. Promoters influence the rate of chemical reaction by improving the efficiency of the catalyst. So, they play an important role in chemical reaction.
4. When few pieces of iron are dropped into a blue coloured copper sulphate solution, the blue colour of the solution fades and eventually turns into green due to the formation of ferrous sulphate.
5. When a solution of slaked lime (calcium hydroxide) is applied to the walls, calcium hydroxide reacts slowly with carbon dioxide present in the atomosphere to form a thin layer of calcium carbonate on the walls of the building.
6. Ammonia is prepared by reaction of nitrogen and hydrogen in the presence of iron and molybdenum. In this case molybdenum acts as a promoter, *i.e.*, it influences the rate of a chemical reaction by improving the efficiency of catalyst (iron).
7. When concentrated sulphuric acid is added to a piece of copper, a blue solution of copper sulphate is formed.
8. When dilute hydrochloric acid (aqueous) is added to calcium carbonate (solid), the carbon dioxide gas is produced which forms bubbles in the liquid, *i.e.*, effervescence takes place.
9. In reaction of iron and copper sulphate, iron is more reactive than copper, so it replaces copper from copper sulphate and thus produces ferrous sulphate and copper.

Chapter 3. Water

1. Marine life exists in the colder regions of the world.
2. Pressure cookers are used in hilly areas also.
3. Quicklime is used for drying NH_3.
4. Air absorbs more water with rising temperature and decreasing moisture.
5. Hard water is used for preparation of beverages and wines.
6. Water is considered as a compound.
7. Ice at 0°C has more cooling effect than water at 0°C.
8. Hard water is not used for washing purpose.
9. Effervescence is seen on opening a soda water bottle.
10. Anhydrous $CaCl_2$ is used in desiccators.
11. Ferric chloride is stored in airtight bottles.
12. Table salt becomes wet and sticky during rainy season. **[February, 2020]**
13. Washing soda loses in weight when exposed to atmosphere.

Ans.

1. The property of anomalous expansion of water enables marine life to exist in the colder regions of the world, because of this phenomenon when the water freezes at the surface, it remains as liquid below the ice layer as density of water is greater than the density of ice and ice is a bad conductor of heat.
2. In the hilly areas water boils at a temperature lower than 100°C with atmospheric pressure being low and so food is not cooked properly there. Therefore, pressure cookers are useful in the hills.

3. Quicklime being basic in nature is suitable for drying NH_3, a basic gas. Basic gas will not react with a base.
4. The higher the temperature of the air, the higher the efflorescence. This is because the air absorbs more water with rising temperature and decreasing moisture.
5. Soft water is free from dissolved salts so it has flat taste. The presence of salts in hard water makes it tasty. So, hard water is used in the preparation of beverages and wines.
6. Water is made up of two elements hydrogen and oxygen, which are in the ratio of 1 : 8 by mass; hence, water is considered as a compound.
7. Ice at 0°C has more cooling effect than water at 0°C because ice at 0°C absorbs 336 J per gram of energy to melt to 0°C water.
8. For washing purpose, soap is used. Soap is chemically a sodium salt of stearic acid. If the water is hard, the calcium and magnesium ions of the water combine with the negative ions of the soap to form a slimy precipitate of insoluble calcium and magnesium, which is termed as soap curd or scum. The formation of soap curd will go on as long as calcium and magnesium ions present there. No soap lather is formed and cleaning of cloth and body will not be possible.
9. Carbon dioxide is dissolved in soda water under high pressure. On opening the bottle, pressure gets released; therefore, the solubility of CO_2 in water decreases and the gas rapidly bubbles out.
10. Anhydrous $CaCl_2$ deliquescent and absorb moisture. So, anhydrous $CaCl_2$ used in desiccator.
11. Ferric chloride is highly deliquescent in nature, *i.e.*, when exposed to atmosphere absorbs moisture and gets converted into its saturated solution. Therefore, it should be stored in airtight bottles.
12. Table salt which is chemically sodium chloride contains the impurities of magnesium chloride which is deliquescent (when exposed to atomosphere, absorbs moisture and gets convereted to saturated solution). Therefore, common salt becomes wet and sticky during rainy season. Sodium chloride is neither hygroscopic nor deliquecent.
13. Washing soda is efflorescent salt (when exposed to atmosphere, loses water of crystallisation and crumbles down to form powder). Thus, it loses weight when exposed to atmosphere.

Chapter 4. Atomic Structure and Chemical Bonding

1. Noble gases exist as monoatoms in a molecule.
2. Non-metals are good oxidising agent.
3. Chemically active atoms have incomplete octet.
4. Ionic compounds are stable.
5. Argon does not react.
6. $^{35}_{17}Cl$ and $^{37}_{17}Cl$ do not differ in their chemical reactions.
7. Actual atomic mass is greater than mass number.
8. Atoms as a whole is an empty space.
9. Rutherford's model of atom could not provide stability to the nucleus.
10. Inert gases are chemical inactive.
11. The physical properties of isotopes are different. **[November, 2019]**
12. Isotopes have the similar chemical properties. **[February, 2020]**

Ans.

1. Elements with valence shell having eight electrons and helium with two electrons cannot gain or lose electrons so they are chemically inactive and are called inert or noble gases. Hence, they exist as monoatoms in a molecule.
2. Non-metals can gain electrons to form ions which are negatively charged. Hence, they are good oxidising agent.
3. The chemical activity of an atom depends upon the number of electrons in the valence shell of its atom. So, atoms having incomplete octet are chemically active.

4. Some repulsive forces between ions is existing in ionic compounds. But, the electrostatic force of attraction between opposite charges is much higher, it makes the ionic compounds stable.
5. Argon is an inert gas so it has zero valency. It is stable and hence does not react.
6. ${}^{35}_{17}Cl$ and ${}^{37}_{17}Cl$ are isotopes of chlorine. Isotopes have same chemical properties but differ in physical properties. So, ${}^{35}_{17}Cl$ and ${}^{37}_{17}Cl$ do not differ in their chemical reactions.
7. Mass number is a whole number approximation of the atomic mass calculated in atomic mass units. So, actual atomic mass is greater than mass number.
8. The size of the nucleus is very small as compared to the size of an atom, therefore atom as a whole is any empty space.
9. According to Rutherford, protons are present inside the nucleus and electrons are revolving around the nucleus. Electron continuously loses energy and ultimately it falls into the nucleus following a spiral path and thus, the nucleus of an atom gets destroyed.
10. Inert gases have complete octet *i.e.*, eight electrons in the outermost shell (except helium which has two electrons), hence they have no tendency to lose, gain or share electrons therefore, they are chemically inert.
11. Isotopes of an element have different number of neutrons hence they have different mass number. As the physical properties depend upon mass number thus, physical properties of isotopes of an element are different.
12. Chemical properties of any element are defined by the number of valence electrons it has, or in other words its atomic number. Isotopes of any element differ in number of neutrons and have same number of electrons and protons, hence the chemical properties of isotopes of any element remain similar.

Chapter 5. The Periodic Table

1. Group I elements are known as alkali metals.
2. As we move down the group atomic size of elements increases.
3. Elements of group I are kept in inert solvent.
4. Helium is used in airships and balloons.
5. Lanthanides and actinides are shown in bottom of the periodic table.
6. Alkali metals and halogens do not occur free in nature.
7. Noble gases do not form compounds readily. **[February, 2020]**
8. The atomic number of an element is more important to the chemist than its relative atomic mass.
9. Group II metals are known as alkaline earth metals.
10. Argon is used to fill light bulbs.
11. Metals act as reducing agents.
12. Non-metals act as oxidising agents.
13. Non-metals form negative ions. **[November, 2019]**

Ans.

1. Alkali metals are the most reactive metals and they react vigorously with water to produce hydrogen and an alkali solution. Hence, they are called as alkali metals.
2. As one move down the group, size of atoms of successive elements increases because of progressive increase in the number of shells.
3. Group I elements are very reactive. Due to its reactive nature, elements of this group are kept in inert solvent like kerosene.
4. Helium is used in airships and balloons because it is both light and unreactive.
5. Lanthanides and actinides have similar properties because they belong to group III B. But they are shown at the bottom of the periodic table because they are large in number and showing them in the main body will distort the shape and layout of the periodic table.

6. Due to their reactive nature alkali metals and halogens do not occur free in nature.
7. The outermost orbital of the inert gases or noble gases are fully occupied. Due to the filled outermost orbital they do not react with others. So, inert gases do not form compounds.
8. Atomic number represents number of electron in an element. Most of the chemical property of an element depends on electrons in their outermost shell which is called as valence shell. Hence, the atomic number is more important to a chemist than its relative atomic mass.
9. Group II metals are known as alkaline earth metals because their oxides occur in the earth's crust and their hydroxides are weak acid.
10. Argon is used to fill light bulbs because argon is a noble gas and it does not react with the filament even at high temperature.
11. Metals can easily lose their outermost 1, 2 or 3 electrons to complete their hence they act as reducing agents.
12. Non-metals can easily gain electrons to complete their outermost octet, act as oxidsing agents.
13. Non-metals have high electron affinity and they accept electrons (usually from metals) to form negative ions easily.

Chapter 6. Hydrogen

1. Concentrated sulphuric acid is not used in preparation of hydrogen gas.
2. Aluminium is not used in laboratory preparation of hydrogen.
3. Hydrogen being a non-metal is included in the activity series of metals.
4. Purified and dried hydrogen is collected over mercury.
5. Potassium is kept in kerosene oil.
6. Though lead is above hydrogen in the activity series, it does not react with dilute hydrochloric acid or dilute sulphuric acid.
7. Potassium and sodium are not used for reaction with dilute hydrochloric acid or dilute sulphuric acid in laboratory preparation of hydrogen.
8. Hydrogen is called inflammable air.
9. Zinc granules are preferred over zinc in the laboratory preparation of hydrogen.
10. Lead is not used with acids to prepare hydrogen gas in the laboratory. **[November, 2019]**

Ans.

1. Concentrated sulphuric acid is not used in preparation of hydrogen gas as it is a strong oxidiser and will produce sulphur dioxide.
2. Aluminium forms a protective coating of Al_2O_3 due to its great affinity for oxygen. Due to coating it does not give hydrogen with acid.
3. Hydrogen though a non-metal, is included in the activity series of metals because it can form a positive ion. Hence, it would occupy a position based on formation of its positive ion.
4. Purified and dried hydrogen is collected over mercury because mercury has no reaction with it.
5. Potassium readily catches fire in air beacuse being alkali metal it reacts with water vapour. So, it is kept in kerosene oil and handled carefully.
6. Though lead is above hydrogen in the activity series, it does not react with dilute hydrochloric acid or dilute sulphuric acid because the surface of metallic lead is protected by a thin layer of lead oxide PbO. This renders the lead essentially insoluble in sulphuric acid.
7. Potassium and sodium are very reactive metals which reacts violently with acids. Thus, they are not used for reaction with dilute hydrochloric acid or dilute sulphuric acid in laboratory preparation of hydrogen.
8. Hydrogen is called inflammable air because of its combustible nature.
9. Zinc granules are preferred over zinc in the laboratory preparation of hydrogen because the impurity present in granulated zinc is copper, whose catalysing effect speeds up the reaction.

10. Lead is not used with acids to prepare hydrogen gas in the laboratory because Lead (Pb) replaces hydrogen from acids giving insoluble salts with acids, which forms a coating on metal surface preventing it from further reaction.

Chapter 7. Study of Gas Laws

1. Gases have neither a fixed volume nor a fixed shape.
2. Gaseous particles in a vessel exert pressure on the walls of the vessel.
3. Mountaineers carry oxygen cylinders with them.
4. Gases are highly compressible.
5. Liquefaction of gases is possible.
6. Gases exert pressure in all direction.
7. Gas completely fills the vessel in which it is kept.
8. Inflating of a balloon is an example which violates the Boyle's Law.
9. Gases have low density than solids or liquids.

Ans.

1. There is negligible force of attraction between the gas molecules. Therefore, the gas molecules are free to move in the entire space available to them; their movement is restricted only by the walls of the container. Thus, they attain the shape of the vessel contained in.
2. Gaseous particles exert pressure on the walls of container in which it is kept because they collide with each other and with the walls of containing vessel. Since, a large number of particles suffer collisions with the wall, an appreciable force acts on the wall.
3. Atomospheric pressure is low at high altitudes, so air is less dense. Hence, a lesser quantity of oxygen is available for breathing. Hence, mountaineers carry oxygen cylinders with them.
4. Gaseous particles have large inter-particle spaces between them. Hence, gases are highly compressible. On applying pressure, the molecules come closer, thus decreasing volume of the gas.
5. On cooling, the kinetic energy of the molecules of a gas is reduced and on applying pressure on a cooled gas the molecules come closer. Hence, the intermolecular space gets reduced and there is an increase in the number of molecules per unit volume. Thus, liquefaction of gases is possible.
6. The number of gas molecules striking the walls of the container per unit time per unit area at the given temperature is same. Thus, gases exerts pressure in all directions.
7. Interparticle space is large or interparticle attraction is weak in gases because the articles are free to move randomly in any direction and takes the shape of the container or vessel in which it is kept.
8. According to Boyle's law :

$$V \propto \frac{1}{P}$$

   Pressure inside the balloon decreases when a balloon is inflated (volume of the gas is decreased) but according to Boyle's law if the is volume is decreasing, pressure should also increase. But this is not happening and hence violates the Boyle's law.
9. Due to the presence of large intermolecular spaces between the molecules, the mass of gas per unit volume is small. That's why gases have low density but in solids or liquids mass is high and intermolecular spaces are negligible.

Chapter 8. Atmospheric Pollution

1. Air pollution affects human, plant and animal lives.
2. Smog is irritating.
3. Oxide of sulphur destroys vegetation and weakens building materials.
4. Acid rain affects soil chemistry.

5. Greenhouse effect has played an important role in the evolution of life on earth.
6. Scrubber helps in reducing the impact of acid rain.
7. Ozone gas is very important for the organisms on earth.
8. Carbon monoxide causes serious health problems.
9. Decaying vegetation by microbes is an example of natural sources of air pollutants.
10. Acid rain impacts on humans also.
11. Greenhouse gases cause global warming. **[November, 2019]**
12. Oxides of nitrogen cause acid rain. **[November, 2019]**

Ans.

1. Air pollution is caused due to the presence of gaseous pollutant like oxides of sulphur, nitrogen, carbon, hydrocarbons and particulate pollutants like dust, smoke, mist, spray and fume which are harmful for survival of lives.
2. Smog reduces visibility, induces respiratory troubles and can cause death by suffocation.
3. Oxides of sulphur are produced by combustion of sulphur containing fuels like coal and oil. It is also produced by metallurgical processes involving sulphide ores which mixes with smoke and fog to form smog, causing harmful to health. It oxidises atmospheric oxygen into SO_3 which combine with water to form sulphuric acid.
4. Acid rain removes calcium and potassium, both the basic ingredients of soil, thus making lose its in feritility, which ultimately damages forests. Acid rain causes loss of nutrients from plants, thus damaging their leaves.
5. Without greenhouse gases, all the heat coming from the sun would have escaped from the earth, which would then become as cold and barren as the moon.
6. Scrubber is a device that absorbs gaseous pollutants. A scrubber used for removing sulphur dioxide from a smoke stack usually consists of a fine spray of water and gas rising from the stack, which is passed through the scrubber, where water absorbs sulphur dioxide. Thus, the formation of this constituent of acid rain is reduced.
7. The ozone layer acts as a blanket in the atomosphere. It absorbs the harmful ultraviolet rays coming from the sun and thus prevents them from reaching the earth. So, ozone layer is very important for the organisms living in earth.
8. Carbon monoxide prevent haemoglobin from carrying oxygen to different parts of the body and causes retardation and dizziness. Thus, it causes serious health problems.
9. Microbial action on organic matter (decaying vegetation) in soil releases pollutant, *i.e.*, nitrous oxide. Hence, it is called a natural source of air pollutant.
10. Acid rain impacts humans too. In sufficiently high concentration it can affect a person's breathing. Sulphur dioxide irritates the upper respiratory tract, the part of the body that serves to expel soot particles and dust from inhaled air. In lower concentrations, it injures lung tissues.
11. Greenhouse gases cause global warming because they absorb the infrared radiations coming from sun and trap the heat in the atmosphere. Hence, by increasing the heat in the atmosphere, greenhouse gases are responsible for the greenhouse effect, which ultimately leads to global warming.
12. Oxides of nitrogen cause acid rain because they react with rain water to produce nitrous and nitric acids, which when mix with rain water produce acid rain.

❑

Observation Based Questions

Give the relevant observation for each of the following:

Chapter 2. Chemical Change and Reaction

1. Silver nitrate is exposed to sunlight.
2. Ammonium dichromate is heated.
3. Zinc is added to copper sulphate solution.
4. Addition of silver nitrate solution to sodium chloride solution. **[February, 2020]**
5. Hydrated copper (II) sulphate is heated.
6. Lead nitrate is heated.
7. H_2S gas is passed through copper sulphate solution.
8. Water is added to quicklime.
9. Ferrous sulphate solution is added to sodium hydroxide solution.
10. Dilute hydrochloric acid is added to calcium carbonate.
11. Action of heat on ammonium chloride. **[November, 2019]**
12. Action of dilute sulphuric acid on zinc carbonate. **[November, 2019]**
13. Sodium carbonate solution is added to calcium chloride solution. **[November, 2019]**
14. Flame test is performed with calcium nitrate. **[February, 2020]**
15. Copper carbonate is decomposed on heating. **[February, 2020]**
16. Dil. H_2SO_4 is added to zinc sulphide. **[February, 2020]**

Ans.

1. When silver nitrate is exposed to sunlight it becomes black as it decomposes to silver, nitrogen dioxide and oxygen.
2. On heating ammonium dichromate it swells and decomposes with flashes of light, evolving nitrogen and water vapour and a green solids, chromium oxide is left behind.
3. The blue colour of copper sulphate solution fades and then becomes colourless. At the same time, reddish brown particles of copper settle down in the beaker.
4. When a solution of silver nitrate is added to a solution of sodium chloride, a white insoluble substance (precipitate) silver chloride is formed.
5. When hydrated copper (II) sulphate is heated in a test tube, the blue coloured crystals changed into white anhydrous salt.
6. When the lead nitrate cystals are heated, they first melt and on further heating gives nitrogen dioxide (a reddish brown gas) and oxygen. Also a yellow solid (PbO) is left behind in the test tube.
7. When H_2S gas is passed through copper sulphate solution, a back precipitate (CuS) is formed.
8. When calcium oxide (quick lime) combines with water, a vigorous reaction takes place with the liberation of a large amount of heat (exothermic reaction), calcium hydroxide, $Ca(OH)_2$ (slaked lime) is formed.
9. When ferrous sulphate solution is added to sodium hydroxide solution, a dirty green precipitate of ferrous hydroxide is formed.
10. When dilute hydrochloric acid is added to calcium carbonate, carbon dioxide is evolved with effervescence.

11. When heated, ammonium chloride decomposes into ammonia and hydrogen chloride :

$$NH_4Cl(s) \rightarrow NH_3(g) + HCl\ (g)$$

12. When zinc carbonate reacts with dil. H_2SO_4, zinc sulphate is obtained along with the

$$ZnCO_3(s) + H_2SO_4(aq) \rightarrow ZnSO_4\ (s) + H_2O(g) + CO_2$$

13. When sodium carbonate solution is added to calcium chloride solution, white precipitate of calcium carbonate is obtained :

$$CaCl_{2(aq)} + Na_2CO_{3(aq)} \rightarrow CaCO_{3(s)} + 2NaCl_{(aq)}$$

14. Calcium nitrate contains Ca^{2+} ions and when subjected to flame test, Ca^{2+} produces deep orange coloured flame.

15. Copper carbonate (green in colour) is decomposed on heating to give cuproous oxide (black in colour) and carbon dioxide gas.

$$\underset{\text{(green)}}{CuCO_3(s)} + \text{heat} \longrightarrow \underset{\text{(black)}}{CuO(s)} + CO_2(g)$$

16. H_2S gas is evolved when dil. H_2SO_4 is added to Zinc sulphide.

$$ZnS(s) + H_2SO_4\ (aq) \longrightarrow Na_2SO_4(aq) + H_2S \uparrow$$

Chapter 3. Water

1. Blue cystals of hydrated copper sulphate are heated in a test tube.
2. Few cystals of pure sodium chloride is heated.
3. Few crystals of potassium nitrate is heated.
4. A burette filled completely with water is inverted over the end of the delivery tube in a trough of water and heated.
5. Anhydrous calcium chloride is exposed to air for sometime. **[November, 2019]**
6. Water is added to anhydrous copper sulphate. **[February, 2020]**

Ans.

1. When blue crystals of hydrated copper sulphate are heated in a test tube, they turn into white powder, which turns back into a blue solid when a few drops of water are added.
2. When few crystals of sodium chloride are heated, they produce a crackling sound called decrepitation. This is due to the breaking of bigger crystals of sodium chloride into smaller ones.
3. When few crystals of potassium nitrate are heated, they first melt into a colourless liquid and then on strong heating they produce oxygen, which rekindles a glowing splint. A light yellow solid (postassium nitrite) is left behind.
4. Gas bubbles are seen escaping from water. They are collected in the graduated tube by downward displacement of water. Thus, water vapour in the gases condense on coming in contact with cold water in the tube.
5. When anhydrous calcium chloride is exposed to air it becomes wet because calcium chloride is deliquescent (hygroscopic) in nature and absorbs water from air.
6. When water is added to anhydrous copper sulphate (white solid), it turns blue in colour as it converts into hydrated copper sulphate, $CuSO_4.5H_2O$ (blue in colour).

Chapter 6. Hydrogen

1. Hydrogen is passed through soap solution.
2. Zinc granules reacts with dilute hydrochloric acid.
3. Burning of magnesium in steam takes place.
4. Calcium reacts with water.

5. Copper oxide is reduced by hydrogen. [November 2019]
6. Magnesium reacts with boiling water.
7. Zinc reacts with water.

Ans.

1. On passing hydrogen gas through soap solution, soap bubbles filled with hydrogen fly higher and burst out. This behaviour proves that hydrogen is lighter than air.
2. When zinc granules react with dilute hydrochloric acid, the reaction gradually start in the form of effervescence and evolution of hydrogen gas takes place.
3. Magnesium burns in steam with an intense white light.
4. When calcium reacts with water, bubbles of hydrogen are liberated and the solution turns milky, turbid and alkaline.
5. On reaction of copper oxide with hydrogen, black colour copper oxide changes to red coloured copper.

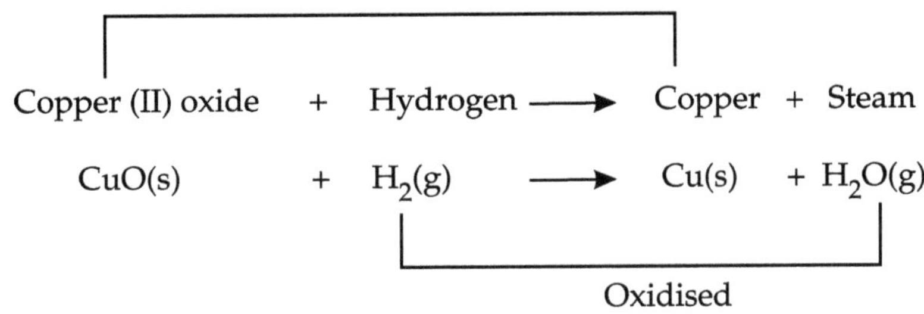

6. Magnesium reacts slowly with boiling water and forms a base, magnesium hydroxide liberating hydrogen gas.
7. Zinc reacts with water to form zinc oxide and hydrogen gas.

❑

Fill in the Blanks

Set 6

Fill in the blanks with the choices given in brackets:

Chapter 1. Language of Chemistry

1. ....is a short form that stands for the atom of a specific element. (Symbol/valency)
2. In naming certain compounds, the suffix 'ate' is used if the number of oxygen atom is.................... . (Two/three)
3. In the potassium chloride, ... is the basic radical. (Chlorine/potassium)
4. The symbol for Gold is............................ . (Ag/Au)
5. Oxygen is a ....anion. (Monovalent/divalent)
6. In sodium chloride, ...is acidic radical. (Sodium/Chlorine)
7. In PCl_3, valency of phosphorus is.......................... . (Three/Five)
8. A molecule is the smalllest particle that has the capability to exist...................... . (Dependently/ Independently)
9. Dalton used symbol of a circle with a dot in its structure to represent..................... (Oxygen/hydrogen)
10. ....suggested that initial letter of an element written in capitals should represent that particular element. (Dalton/Jons Jakob Berzelius)
11. The molecular formula of Aluminium Oxide is...................(AlO_3/Al_2O_3). **[February, 2020]**

Ans. 1. Symbol, 2. Three, 3. Potassium, 4. Au,
5. Divalent, 6. Chlorine 7. Three, 8. Independently,
9. Hydrogen 10. Jons Jakob Berzelius. 11. Al_2O_3

Chapter 2. Chemical Change and Reaction

1. A chemical bond is a..............................that holds the atoms of a molecule together, as in a compound. (force/arrangement).
2. In..........................reaction, molecules of the reactants adsorb light energy to get activated and then react rapidly. (photolysis/thermal decomposition)
3. Phosphoric acid is an example of..........................catalyst. (positive/negative)
4. Digestion of food by our body is an example of..............................reaction. (decomposition, neutralisation)
5. Acid that is accidentally spilled on our clothes or body can be neutralised with............................solution. (ammonia/formic acid)
6. The least reactive non-metal is..........................(iodine/bromine)
7. On heating, hydrated copper sulphate changes its colour from..........................to white. (black/blue)
8. When insoluble substance is formed in a chemical reaction, it is called as.......................... . (effervescence/ precipitate)
9. Acetylene breaks up into carbon and hydrogen by absorbing........................... energy. (light/sound)
10. The promoter used in production of ammonia is.......................... . (molybdenum/iron)
11. A carbonate that does not decompose on heating is .... (K_2CO_3/$CaCO_3$) **[February, 2020]**

Ans. 1. Force 2. Photolysis 3. Negative 4. Decomposition
5. Ammonia 6. Iodine 7. Blue 8. Precipitate
9. Sound 10. Molybdenum 11. K_2CO_3

Chapter 3. Water

1. In.........................process solubility of solute increases with increase of temperature. (endothermic/ exothermic)
2. Solubility of solids in water usually increases with rise in......................... . (pressure/temperature)
3. ....is called as universal solvent. (Water/Alcohol)
4. Aquatic plants make use of dissolved......................... for photosynthesis. (carbon dioxide/oxygen)
5. The boiling point of water.........................due to the presence of dissolved impurities in it. (increases/ decreases)
6. Marine life, like fish use.............................of air dissolved in water for their cellular respiration. (oxygen/ water vapour)
7. In the solid solution of brass.........................acts as solvent. (copper/zinc)
8. .... checks the poisoning of water by lead pipes. (Soft water/Hard water)
9. Water that contains only.........................of calcium and magnesium is called temporary hard water. (hydrogen carbonates/sulphates)
10. Pure water boils at......................... . (100°C/0°C)

Ans. 1. Endothermic process 2. Pressure 3. Water 4. Carbon dioxide 5. Increases 6. Oxygen 7. Copper 8. Hard water 9. Hydrogen carbonates 10. 100°C.

Chapter 4. Atomic Structure and Chemical Bonding

1. The bonds formed between metals and non-metals are...................bonds. (covalent/electrovalent)
2. To attain the stable electronic configuration of the nearest noble gas, chlorine needs......................... electron. (one/two)
3. Electropositive atom loses electrons and undergoes......................... .(oxidation/reduction)
4. In covalent bond formation each atoms contribute.............................number of electrons. (equal/ unequal)
5. Covalency of nitrogen is .... (two/three)
6. Ethene molecule is .... (single bonded/double bonded)
7. Electrovalent compounds have.........................boiling point. (low/high)
8. Hydrogen is a......................... (metal/non-metal)
9. The type of bonding in calcium oxide is......................... . (electrovalent/covalent)
10. The chemical properties of an element are decided by......................... . (number of electrons/valence electrons).

Ans. 1. Electrovalent bond 2. One 3. Oxidation 4. Equal 5. Three 6. Double bonded 7. High 8. Non-metal 9. Electrovalent 10. Valence electrons.

Chapter 5. The Periodic Table

1. According to the Modern Periodic Law, physical and chemical properties of element are periodic functions of their.......................(atomic weight/atomic numbers). **[February, 2020]**
2. Group II metals are called.......................metals. (alkali/alkaline earth) **[February, 2020]**
3. The vertical columns in the periodic table are.........................(groups/periods) **[February, 2020]**
4. .... is the longest period in the periodic table. (Period 6/Period 7)
5. Reactivity of elements decreases up to.........................and then increases. (group 12/group 14)
6. Going across a period left to right, atomic size......................... . (decreases/increases)

7. In modern periodic table, there are.........................horizontal rows. (seven/eighteen)
8. Lanthanides and actinides are called as.........................elements. (transition/inner trasition)
9. The outermost orbit of *s*-block elements is......................... . (complete/incomplete)
10. In periodic table, the sixth period contains.........................elements. (32/8)
11. Potassium has.........................valence electrons. (one/two)
12. The least reactive halogen is......................... (iodine/chlorine)
13. The number of elements in period 1 is......................... . (two/eight) **[November, 2019]**
14. Modern Periodic Table has......................... groups. (eight/eighteen) **[November, 2019]**
15. Halogens are placed in group.................. (17/18) **[November, 2019]**
16. ....is a highly radioactive and rare element. (Astatine/Bromine)
17. The number of electrons in the valence shell of an atom represents its......................... . (group/period) **[November, 2019]**
18. .... elements are present on the right side of the periodic table. (Metallic/Non-metallic) **[November, 2019]**

Ans. 1. Atomic number 2. Alkaline 3. groups 4. Period 6
5. Group 14 6. Increases 7. Seven 8. Inner transition
9. Incomplete 10. 32 11. One 12. Iodine
13. two 14. eighteen 15. 17 16. Astatine
17. Group 18. Non-metallic

Chapter 6. Hydrogen

1. Hydrogen is a very.........................gas. (heavy/light)
2. Most preferred metal in laboratory production of hydrogen is......................... . (aluminium/zinc)
3. ....is an example of liquid reducing agent. (Hydrogen sulphide/Hydrogen peroxide)
4. ....is used in production of hydrogen in a large scale. (Haber's process/Bosch process)
5. Hydrogen acts as.........................agent on reacting with non-metals. (oxidising/reducing)
6. In laboratory preparation of hydrogen,.........................is most preferred metal. (copper/zinc)
7. ....do not displace hydrogen from dilute acid. (gold, sodium)
8. ....is the one of the impurity present with hydrogen in its laboratory preparation. (Hydrogen sulphide/Carbon monoxide)
9. ....is an example of liquid oxidising agent. (Hydrogen peroxide/Hydrogen sulphide)
10. Ammonia is an example of.........................reducing agent. (liquid/gaseous)

Ans. 1. Light 2. Zinc 3. Hydrogen Sulphide 4. Bosch process
5. Reducing 6. Zinc 7. Gold 8. Hydrogen sulphide
9. Hydrogen peroxide 10. Gaseous.

Chapter 7. Study of Gas Laws

1. The average kinetic energy of a particle is.........................proportional to its absolute temperature. (directly/inversely)
2. Gases can be.........................on cooling. (solidified/liquefied)
3. S.I. unit of pressure is......................... . (pascal/kelvin)
4. At constant pressure, volume of a given mass of gas is directly proportional to.........................by Charles' law. (temperature/surface area)
5. The temperature.........................is called absolute zero. (–273°C, 273°C)
6. ....would reduce to half if temperature is reduced to half. (Pressure/Volume)
7. Standard pressure in terms of cm Hg is......................... . (760/76)

8. The relationship between volume-temperatue is given by.......................... . (Boyle/Charles)
9. Volume of the gas is..........................proportional to the pressure at constant temperature. (inversely/directly)
10. The PV vs P graph for a gas a.......................... . (straight line parallel to the x-axis/parabola)
11. By increasing the presure on the volume of an enclosed gas at constant (i)....................., the volume of the gas (ii)........................ . This is given by (iii) .... law. **[February, 2020]**

Ans. 1. Directly 2. Liquefied 3. Pascal 4. Temperature
5. –273°C 6. Volume 7. 76 cm Hg 8. Charles
9. Directly 10. Straight line parallel to *x*-axis
11. (i) temperature (ii) decreases (iii) Boyle's law

Chapter 8. Atmospheric Pollution

1. Locking of chlorine monoxide and free radicals of chlorine is called.......................... . (scavenging/chlorination)
2. Ozone is a poisonous gas with a..........................like smell. (methane/chlorine)
3. Toxic and otherwise harmful substances that have an undesirable impact on different components of the environment and life forms are known as.......................... . (green housegas/pollutants)
4. Ozone is formed by the action of.......................... of the sun. (ultraviolet rays/methane gas)
5. In sunlight, nitrogen dioxide oxidises hydrocarbons to form.......................... . (photochemical smog/chloro-fluoro-carbon)
6. The main source of water vapour is burning of.......................... . (hydrocarbons/carbond dioxide)
7. ....is one of the green house gases. (oxygen/carbon dioxide)
8. The chemical that is produced due to anaerobic decomposition of organic matter is soil is..................... . (nitric acid/methane)
9. Internal combustion of engines produces .... (nitrogen oxide/nitric acid)
10. Ozone layer depletes due to extensive use of.......................... . (CFC/ozone)

Ans. 1. Scavenging 2. Chlorine 3. Pollutants 4. Ultraviolet rays
5. Photochemical smog 6. Hydrocarbons 7. Carbon dioxide 8. Methane
9. Nitrogen oxide 10. CFC.

❑

Match the Columns

Set 7

Match the following:

Chapter 1. Language of Chemistry

1.

COLUMN A	COLUMN B
(i) Element whose atomic mass is taken as standard unit in measurement of atomic mass of other elements.	(a) Sodium hypochlorite
(ii) Chemical name of $NaClO$	(b) C-12
(iii) Chemical name of $NaClO_2$	(c) Sodium chlorite
(iv) Element possess variable valency	(d) Chlorine
(v) Element possess valency of 1	(e) Mercury

Ans.

COLUMN A	COLUMN B
(i) Element whose atomic mass is taken as standard unit in measurement of atomic mass of other elements.	(b) C-12
(ii) Chemical name of $NaClO$	(a) Sodium hypochlorite
(iii) Chemical name of $NaClO_2$	(c) Sodium chlorite
(iv) Element possess variable valency	(e) Mercury
(v) Element possess valency of 1	(d) Chlorine

2.

COLUMN A	COLUMN B
(i) Sodium carbonate	(a) NH_3
(ii) Potassium hydroxide	(b) H_2SO_4
(iii) Ammonia	(c) KOH
(iv) Methane	(d) Na_2CO_3
(v) Sulphuric acid	(e) CH_4

Ans.

COLUMN A	COLUMN B
(i) Sodium carbonate	(d) Na_2CO_3
(ii) Potassium hydroxide	(c) KOH
(iii) Ammonia	(a) NH_3
(iv) Methane	(e) CH_4
(v) Sulphuric acid	(b) H_2SO_4

Chapter 2. Chemical Change and Reaction

1.

COLUMN A	COLUMN B
(i) Formation of glucose	(a) Blue
(ii) Production of ammonia	(b) Photochemical reaction
(iii) Colour of $CuSO_4$	(c) Sound energy
(iv) Colour of ferrous hydroxide	(d) Molybdenum
(v) Decomposition of acetylene	(e) Dirty green

Ans.

COLUMN A	COLUMN B
(i) Formation of glucose	(b) Photochemical reaction
(ii) Production of ammonia	(d) Molybdenum
(iii) Colour of $CuSO_4$	(a) Blue
(iv) Colour of ferrous hydroxide	(e) Dirty green
(v) Decomposition of acetylene	(c) Sound energy

2.

COLUMN A	COLUMN B
(i) Phosphoric acid	(a) Light energy
(ii) Molybdenum	(b) Exothermic reaction
(iii) Photosynthesis	(c) Promoter
(iv) Magnesium	(d) White light
(v) Respiration	(e) Negative catalyst

Ans.

COLUMN A	COLUMN B
(i) Phosphoric acid	(e) Negative catalyst
(ii) Molybdenum	(c) Promoter
(iii) Photosynthesis	(a) Light energy
(iv) Magnesium	(d) White light
(v) Respiration	(b) Exothermic reaction

3.

COLUMN A (processes)	COLUMN B (Products)
(i) Phosphoric acid	(a) $Na + Cl_2$
(ii) Molybdenum	(b) $NaCl + H_2O$
(iii) Photosynthesis	(c) $Ca(OH)_2$
(iv) Magnesium	(d) $CaO + CO_2$
(v) Respiration	(e) $BaSO_4 + NaCl$

Ans.

COLUMN A	COLUMN B
(i) Combination	(c) $Ca(OH)_2$
(ii) Thermal decomposition	(d) $CaO + CO_2$
(iii) Electroysis	(a) $Na + Cl_2$
(iv) Precipitation	(e) $BaSO_4 + NaCl$
(v) Neutralisation	(b) $NaCl + H_2O$

Chapter 3. Water

1.

COLUMN A	COLUMN B
(i) Efflorescent substance	(a) Caustic potash
(ii) Deliquescent substance	(b) Dry sodium sulphate
(iii) Drying agents	(c) Washing soda
(iv) Hygroscopic substance	(d) Conc. sulphuric acid
(v) Dehydrating agent	(e) Silica gel

Ans.

COLUMN A	COLUMN B
(i) Efflorescent substance	(c) Washing soda
(ii) Deliquescent substance	(a) Caustic potash
(iii) Drying agents	(b) Dry sodium sulphate
(iv) Hygroscopic substance	(e) Silica gel
(v) Dehydrating agent	(d) Conc. sulphuric acid

2.

COLUMN A	COLUMN B
(i) Epsom salt	(a) Hydrated potassium aluminium sulphate
(ii) Gypsum	(b) Copper (II) sulphate heptahydrate
(iii) Plaster of Paris	(c) Magnesium sulphate heptahydrate
(iv) Potash alum	(d) Calcium sulphate dihydrate
(v) Blue vitriol	(e) Calcium sulphate hemihydrate

Ans.

COLUMN A	COLUMN B
(i) Epsom salt	(c) Magnesium sulphate heptahydrate
(ii) Gypsum	(d) Calcium sulphate dihydrate
(iii) Plaster of Paris	(e) Calcium sulphate hemihydrate
(iv) Potash alum	(a) Hydrated potassium aluminium sulphate
(v) Blue vitriol	(b) Copper (II) sulphate heptahydrate

3.

COLUMN A	COLUMN B
(i) Quick lime	(a) Specific value of latent heat of vaporisation of water
(ii) 336 J/g	(b) Deliquescence substance
(iii) 540 cal/g	(c) Efflorescent substance
(iv) Washing soda	(d) Hygroscopic substance
(v) Magnesium chloride	(e) Specific value of latent heat of fusion of ice

Ans.

COLUMN A	COLUMN B
(i) Quick lime	(d) Hygroscopic substance
(ii) 336 J/g	(e) Specific value of latent heat of fusion of ice
(iii) 540 cal/g	(a) Specific value of latent heat of vaporisation of water
(iv) Washing soda	(c) Efflorescent substance
(v) Magnesium chloride	(b) Deliquescence substance

Chapter 4. Atomic Structure and Chemical Bonding

1.

COLUMN A	COLUMN B
(i) Zero valency	(a) Magnesium
(ii) Good reducing agent	(b) Helium
(iii) Isotope	(c) Chlorine
(iv) Valency four	(d) Hydrogen
(v) Neutron absent	(e) Carbon

Ans.

COLUMN A	COLUMN B
(i) Zero valency	(b) Helium
(ii) Good reducing agent	(a) Magnesium
(iii) Isotope	(c) Chlorine
(iv) Valency four	(e) Carbon
(v) Neutron absent	(d) Hydrogen

2.

COLUMN A	COLUMN B
(i) Covalent compounds	(a) Triple bond
(ii) Nitrogen	(b) Chlorine
(iii) Neon	(c) Low boiling point
(iv) Oxidising agent	(d) Helium
(v) Duplet	(e) Inert gas

Ans.

COLUMN A	COLUMN B
(i) Covalent compounds	(c) Low boiling point
(ii) Nitrogen	(a) Triple bond
(iii) Neon	(e) Inert gas
(iv) Oxidising agent	(b) Chlorine
(v) Duplet	(d) Helium

3.

COLUMN A (Discoverer or scientist)	COLUMN B (Related discovery or theory)
(i) John Dalton	(a) Nucleus
(ii) E Goldstein	(b) Electron
(iii) J Chadwick	(c) Proton
(iv) J.J. Thomson	(d) Neutron
	(e) Indivisibility of atom

Ans.

COLUMN A (Discoverer or scientist)	COLUMN B (Related discovery or theory)
(i) John Dalton	(e) Indivisibility
(ii) E Goldstein	(c) Proton
(iii) J Chadwick	(d) Neutron
(iv) J.J. Thomson	(b) Electron

4.

COLUMN A (Element)	COLUMN B (Valency)
(i) Oxygen	(a) 1
(ii) Potassium	(b) 2
(iii) Nitrogen	(c) 3
(iv) Silicon	(d) 4

Ans.

COLUMN A (Element)	COLUMN B (Valency
(i) Oxygen	(b) 2
(ii) Potassium	(a) 1
(iii) Nitrogen	(c) 3
(iv) Silicon	(d) 4

5.

COLUMN A ((Experiments)	COLUMN B (Conducted by)
(i) Cathode rays experiment	(a) Mulliken
(ii) Gold foil experiment	(b) Goldstein
(iii) Anode rays experiment	(c) Thomson
	(d) Rutherford
	(e) Neils Bohr

Ans.

COLUMN A (Experiments)	COLUMN B (Conducted by)
(i) Cathode rays experiment	(c) Thomson
(ii) Gold foil experiment	(d) Rutherford
(iii) Anode rays experiment	(b) Goldstein

Chapter 5. The Periodic Table

1.

COLUMN A	COLUMN B
(i) Balloons	(a) Argon
(ii) Radioactive elements	(b) Group I
(iii) Most reactive non-metals	(c) Helium
(iv) Most reactive metals	(d) Actinides
(v) Bulb	(e) Group 17

Ans.

COLUMN A	COLUMN B
(i) Balloons	(c) Helium
(ii) Highly reactive metals	(d) Actinides
(iii) Most reactive non-metals	(e) Group 17
(iv) Most reactive metals	(b) Group I
(v) Bulb	(a) Argon

2.

COLUMN A	COLUMN B
(i) Electrons short by one electron in octet	(a) Transition element
(ii) Highly reactive metals	(b) Noble gases
(iii) Non-reactive elements	(c) Alkali metals
(iv) Elements of group 3 to 12	(d) Alkaline earth metals
(v) Radioactive elements	(e) Halogens
(vi) Elements with two electrons in the outermost orbit	(f) Actinides

Ans.

COLUMN A	COLUMN B
(i) Electrons short by one electron in octet	(e) Halogens
(ii) Highly reactive metals	(c) Alkali metals
(iii) Non-reactive elements	(b) Noble gases
(iv) Elements of group 3 to 12	(a) Transition element
(v) Radioactive elements	(f) Actinides
(vi) Elements with two electrons in the outermost orbit	(d) Alkaline earth metals

3. **[February, 2020]**

COLUMN A	COLUMN B
(i) Liquid metal	(a) Bromine
(ii) An element without neutron	(b) Mercury
(iii) An oxidising agent	(c) Helium
(iv) A liquid non-metal	(d) Hydrogen
(v) An inert gas	(e) Oxygen

Ans.

COLUMN A	COLUMN B
(i) Liquid metal	(b) Mercury
(ii) An element without neutron	(d) Hydrogen
(iii) An oxidising agent	(e) Oxygen
(iv) A liquid non-metal	(a) Bromine
(v) An inert gas	(c) Helium

Chapter 6. Hydrogen

1.

COLUMN A	COLUMN B
(i) Concentrated sulphuric acid	(a) Hydrogen
(ii) Pop sound	(b) Inert solvent
(iii) Impurities	(c) Potassium
(iv) Alkali metals	(d) Drying agent
(v) Most reactive metal	(e) Silver nitrate

Ans.

COLUMN A	COLUMN B
(i) Concentrated sulphuric acid	(d) Drying agent
(ii) Pop sound	(a) Hydrogen
(iii) Impurities	(e) Silver nitrate
(iv) Alkali metals	(b) Inert solvent
(v) Most reactive metal	(c) Potassium

2.

COLUMN A	COLUMN B
(i) Bosch process	(a) Sulphur dioxide
(ii) Least reactive metal	(b) Chlorine
(iii) Impurities in laboratory production of hydrogen	(c) Hydrogen
(iv) Oxidising agent	(d) Ammonia
(v) Reducing agent	(e) Gold

Ans.

COLUMN A	COLUMN B
(i) Bosch process	(c) Hydrogen
(ii) Least reactive metal	(e) Gold
(iii) Impurities in laboratory production of hydrogen	(a) Sulphur dioxide
(iv) Oxidising agent	(b) Chlorine
(v) Reducing agent	(d) Ammonia

3.

COLUMN A	COLUMN B
(i) An isotope of hydrogen	(a) Aluminium
(ii) Less reactive metal than hydrogen	(b) Potassium
(iii) Form amphoteric oxides	(c) Tritium
(iv) Form alkali	(d) Platinum

Ans.

COLUMN A	COLUMN B
(i) An isotope of hydrogen	(a) Tritium
(ii) Less reactive metal than hydrogen	(d) Platinum
(iii) Form amphotenric oxides	(a) Aluminium
(iv) Form alkali	(b) Potassium

4.

COLUMN I	COLUMN II
(i) Aluminium	(a) Does not displace hydrogen
(iii) Copper	(b) Used in laboratory preparation of hydrogen
(iii) Potassium	(c) Form amphoteric oxide
(iv) Zinc	(d) Most reactive metal
(v) Tritium	(e) Radioactive in nature

Ans.

COLUMN A	COLUMN B
(i) Aluminium	(c) Form amphoteric oxide
(iii) Copper	(a) Does not displace hydrogen
(iii) Potassium	(d) Most reactive metal
(iv) Zinc	(b) Used in laboratory preparation of hydrogen
(v) Tritium	(e) Radioactive in nature

5.

COLUMN A	COLUMN B
(i) Hydrogen sulphide	(a) Bosch process
(ii) Ammonia	(b) Oxidation product
(iii) Hydrogen	(c) Strong affinity for hydrogen
(iv) Water	(d) Rotten egg smell
(v) Chlorine	(e) Haber's process

Ans.

COLUMN A	COLUMN B
(i) Hydrogen sulphide	(d) Rotten egg smell
(ii) Ammonia	(e) Haber's process
(iii) Hydrogen	(a) Bosch process
(iv) Water	(b) Oxidation product
(v) Chlorine	(c) Strong affinity for hydrogen

6. [November, 2019]

COLUMN A	COLUMN B
(i) Zinc	(a) Most active metal
(ii) Iron	(b) Has no reaction with dilute acid
(iii) Copper	(c) Reacts with cold water forming milky solution
(iv) Potassium	(d) Amphoteric metal
(v) Calcium	(e) Has valencies of 2 and 3

Ans.

COLUMN A	COLUMN B
(i) Zinc	(d) Amphoteric metal
(ii) Iron	(e) Has valencies of 2 and 3
(iii) Copper	(b) Has no reaction with dilute acid
(iv) Potassium	(a) Most active metal
(v) Calcium	(c) Reacts with cold water forming milky solution

Chapter 7. Study of Gas Laws

1.

COLUMN A	COLUMN B
(i) 1 atm	(a) Constant temperature
(ii) Isotherm	(b) –273°C
(iii) Isobar	(c) 760 mm Hg
(iv) Zero Kelvin	(d) Pascal
(v) Pressure	(e) Constant pressure

Ans.

COLUMN A	COLUMN B
(i) 1 atm	(c) 760 mm Hg
(ii) Isotherm	(a) Constant temperature
(iii) Isobar	(e) Constant pressure
(iv) Zero Kelvin	(b) –273°C
(v) Pressure	(d) Pascal

2.

COLUMN A	COLUMN B
(i) cm^3	(a) $V/T = V_1/T_1$
(ii) Torr	(b) Volume
(iii) Charle's Law	(c) $PV = P_1V_1$
(iv) Kelvin	(d) Pressure
(v) Boyle's Law	(e) Temperature

Ans.

COLUMN A	COLUMN B
(i) cm^3	(b) Volume
(ii) Torr	(d) Pressure
(iii) Charles' Law	(a) $V/T = V_1/T_1$
(iv) Kelvin	(e) Temperature
(v) Boyle's Law	(c) $PV = P_1V_1$

3.

COLUMN A	COLUMN B
(i) Boyle's law	(a) – 273°C
(ii) Charles' law	(b) $\frac{V_1}{T_1} = \frac{V_2}{T_1}$
(iii) Ideal gas equation	(c) $p_1V_1 = p_2V_2$
(iv) Absolute zero	(d) $\frac{p_1V_1}{T_1} = \frac{p_2V_2}{T_2}$

Ans.

COLUMN A	COLUMN B
(i) Boyle's law	(c) $p_1V_1 = p_2V_2$
(ii) Charles' law	(b) $\frac{V_1}{T_1} = \frac{V_2}{T_1}$
(iii) Ideal gas equation	(d) $\frac{p_1V_1}{T_1} = \frac{p_2V_2}{T_2}$
(iv) Absolute zero	(a) – 273°C

4.

COLUMN A (Graphical representation)	COLUMN B (X and Y coordinates)
(i) 	(a) pV *vs* V
(ii) 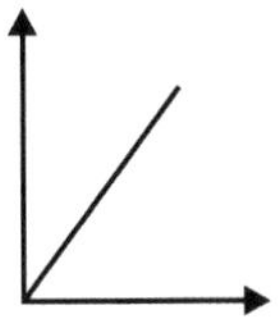	(b) p *vs* V
(iii) 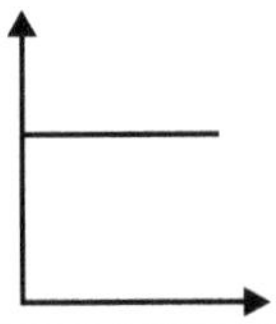	(c) p *vs* $\frac{1}{V}$

Ans.

COLUMN A (Graphical representation)	COLUMN B (X and Y coordinates)
(i) 	(b) p *vs* V
(ii) 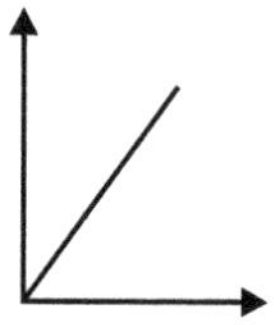	(c) p *vs* $\frac{1}{V}$
(iii) 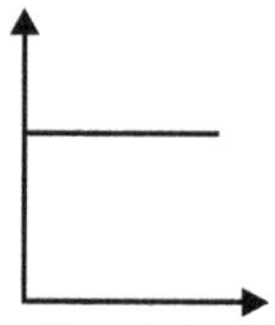	(a) pV *vs* V

5.

COLUMN A (Temperature in Celsius)	COLUMN B (Temperature in Kelvin)
(i) 17°C	(a) 273 k
(ii) 20°C	(b) 0 K
(iii) – 273°C	(c) 290 K
(iv) 273°C	(d) 293 K
(v) 0°C	(e) 546 K

Ans.

COLUMN A (Temperature in Celsius)	COLUMN B (Temperature in Kelvin)
(i) 17°C	(c) 290 K
(ii) 20°C	(d) 293 K
(iii) – 273°C	(b) 0 K
(iv) 273°C	(e) 546 K
(v) 0°C	(a) 273 k

Chapter 8. Atmospheric Pollution

1.

COLUMN A	COLUMN B
(i) Tobacco Smoke	(a) Used as fuel
(ii) Asthma	(b) Carbon monoxide poisoning
(iii) TEL (Tetraethyl lead)	(c) Lung fibrosis
(iv) Carbon monoxide	(d) Affects yield of crops
(v) Sulphur dioxide	(e) Prevents haemoglobin

(vi) Carboxy haemoglobin	(f) Comes from cotton dust
(vii) Hydrogen sulphide	(g) Reduces oxygen carrying capacity
(viii) Carbon monoxide	(h) Irritation to human eyes
(ix) CNG	(i) Lung cancer
(x) Cotton dust	(j) Come from motor vehicles

Ans.

COLUMN A	COLUMN B
(i) Tobacco Smoke	(i) Lung cancer
(ii) Asthma	(f) Comes from cotton dust
(iii) TEL (Tetraethyl lead)	(j) Come from motor vehicles
(iv) Carbon monoxide	(e) Prevents haemoglobin
(v) Sulphur dioxide	(d) Affects yield of crops
(vi) Carboxy haemoglobin	(b) Carbon monoxide poisoning
(vii) Hydrogen sulphide	(h) Irritation to human eyes
(viii) Carbon monoxide	(g) Reduces oxygen carrying capacity
(ix) CNG	(a) Used as fuel
(x) Cotton dust	(c) Lung fibrosis

2.

COLUMN A	COLUMN B
(a) $4NO_2 + 2H_2O + O_2 \rightarrow$	(i) $2SO_3$
(b) $2SO_2 + O_2 \xrightarrow{\text{Particulate}}$	(ii) H_2SO_4
(c) $SO_2 + H_2O \rightarrow$	(iii) O_3
(d) $O + O_2 \underset{\text{light}}{\overset{\text{UV}}{\rightleftharpoons}}$	(iv) $4HNO_3$

Ans.

COLUMN A	COLUMN B
(a) $4NO_2 + 2H_2O + O_2 \rightarrow$	(iv) $4HNO_3$
(b) $2SO_2 + O_2 \xrightarrow{\text{Particulate}}$	(i) $2SO_3$
(c) $SO_2 + H_2O \rightarrow$	(ii) H_2SO_4
(d) $O + O_2 \underset{\text{light}}{\overset{\text{UV}}{\rightleftharpoons}}$	(iii) O_3

❑

Identify the Gas or Substance | Set 8 |

Identify the gas or substance:

Chapter 2. Chemical Change and Reaction

1. A carbonate which does not decompose on heating.
2. A nitrate which produces oxygen as the only gas.
3. A compound which produces carbon dioxide on heating.
4. A nitrate which produces brown gas on heating.
5. A carbonate which produces yellow residue.
6. A nitrate that gives nitrogen dixoide and oxygen gas on heating.
7. A gas that is produced due to heating of ammonium dichromate.
8. A hydrated compound which changes from blue to white on heating.
9. A metal which is most reactive metal.
10. A basic gas which turn red litmus solution blue. **[February, 2020]**
11. A gas that reacts with hydrochloric acid to produce solid ammonium chloride.

Ans. **1.** Sodium carbonate **2.** Potassium nitrate **3.** Calcium carbonate
4. Lead nitrate **5.** Zinc carbonate **6.** Lead nitrate
7. Nitrogen **8.** Hydrated copper sulphate ($CuSO_4.5H_2O$) **9.** Sodium
10. Ammonia **11.** Ammonia gas

Chapter 3. Water

1. The substance which causes permanent hardness in water. **[November, 2019]**
2. A salt the solubility of which increases rapidly with rise of temperature. **[November, 2019]**
3. The substance having more than negligible but less than high solubility.
4. The substance obtained on heating blue vitriol crystals.
5. Reactant added to hard water due to which bicarbonates of calcium and magnesium are precipitated.
6. A reddish-brown gas liberated on heating lead nitrate crystals. **[February, 2020]**

Ans.

1. Calcium sulphate ($CaSO_4$) **2.** Sodium chloride (NaCl)
3. Calcium hydroxide ($Ca(OH)_2$)
4. White amorphous copper sulphate ($CuSO_4$) and water (H_2O)
5. Lime (CaO) **6.** Nitrogen dioxide

Chapter 4. Atomic Structure and Chemical Bonding

1. An element having zero valency.
2. Metal with valency one.
3. Atoms of the same element differing in mass number.
4. Elements having same mass number but differnt atomic number.

5. The element which does not contain any neutron in its nucleus.
6. A metal with valency two.
7. An element with electronic configuration of 2, 8, 7.
8. Molecules of some elements are one in atom.

Ans. 1. Helium 2. Sodium 3. Protium and deuterium
4. Argon and calcium (both have mass number 40) 5. Hydrogen
6. Magnesium 7. Chlorine 8. Inert gas

Chapter 5. The Periodic Table

1. A noble gas with duplet arrangement of electrons.
2. A metalloid in period 3.
3. An element with valency 2.
4. A noble gas having electronic configuration of 2, 8, 8.
5. A group whose elements have zero valency.
6. An alkaline earth metal in period 3
7. An alkali metal in period 3 that dissolves in water giving a strong alkali.
8. A typical element of group 14.
9. An non-metal present in period 3.
10. A noble gas of period 3.
11. The metal which is least reactive.

Ans. 1. Helium 2. Silicon 3. Magnesium
4. Argon 5. Group 18 6. Magnesium
7. Sodium 8. Silicon 9. Silicon
10. Argon 11. Gold

Chapter 6. Hydrogen

1. An oxidising agent that does not contain oxygen.
2. A substance that will reduce aqueous iron (III) ions to iron (II) ions.
3. A liquid that is an oxidising as well as reducing agent.
4. A gas that is oxidising as well as reducing agent.
5. A solid that is an oxidising agent.
6. A metal which is preferred in producing of hydrogen from acid.
7. A metal which is used to collect hydrogen.
8. An acid which is good drying agent.
9. A non-metal included in activity series of metals.
10. A greenish yellow gas that turns moist starch iodide paper blue black. **[February, 2020]**
11. A gas which burns in air or oxygen forming water. **[February, 2020]**
12. A gas that turns lead acetate paper balck. **[February, 2020]**
13. A gas that turns orange potassium dichromate paper green. **[February, 2020]**
14. A colourless odourless gas that relights a glowing splint. **[February, 2020]**

Ans. 1. Chlorine 2. Hydrogen sulphide 3. Water
4. Hydrogen gas 5. Managanese dioxide 6. Zinc
7. Mercury 8. Concentrated sulphuric acid 9. Hydrogen
10. Chlorine 11. Hydrogen
12. The gas that turns lead acetate paper black is hydrogen sulphide :

$$H_2S + Pb(CH_3COO)_2 \longrightarrow PbS + 2CH_3COOH$$

Hydrogen sulphide — Lead sulphide (Black)

13. Sulphur dioxide (SO_2) is the gas which turns potassium dichromate paper green :

$$K_2Cr_2O_7 + 3SO_2 + H_2SO_4 \longrightarrow Cr_2(SO_4)_3 + K_2SO_4 + H_2O$$

Potassium dichromate (Orange colour) — Chromium sulphate (Green colour)

14. Oxygen

Chapter 8. Atmospheric Pollution

1. Gases that release from coal power plants.
2. A gas that causes irritation of human eyes.
3. A substance that affects teeth.
4. A gas that affects yield of crops.
5. A gas that reduces growth of crops.
6. A substance that formed by reaction between atomospheric nitrogen and oxygen in the presence of electric discharge, which happens during thunder storms.
7. A gas that causes irritation in mucous membrane.
8. A gas that produced by decaying organic matter.
9. A hydrocarbon which contributes towards the greenhouse effect. **[February, 2020]**
10. A gas that causes acid rain. **[February, 2020]**
11. A gas that is formed by the action of violet rays of the sun on oxygen. **[November, 2019]**
12. Gas that combines with haemoglobin and form carboxy haemoglobin.
13. A substance that formed when oxides of nitrogen and sulphur come into contact with rain water.

Ans. **1.** Carbon monoxide, sulphur dioxide **2.** Hydrogen sulphide **3.** Fluoride
4. Sulphur dioxide **5.** Hydrogen sulphide **6.** Nitric oxide
7. Nitrogen dioxide **8.** Hydrogen sulphide **9.** Methane

10. Nitrogen dioxide is one gas causing acid rain, the chemical equation is as follows :

$$2NO_2 + H_2O \longrightarrow HNO_2 + HNO_3$$

Nitrogen dioxide — Nitrous acid — Nitric acid

11. Ozone (O_3) **12.** Carbon monoxide
13. Acid rain

❑

Distinguish Between

Set 9

Distinguish between the following:

Chapter 1. Language of Chemistry

1. Sodium and Helium (valency)
2. Ozone and Nitrogen (atomicity)
3. Oxygen and Carbon (atomic mass)
4. Ferrous oxide and Ferric oxide (chemical formula)
5. Potassium and Phosphorus (Symbol)
6. Valency and Variable valency
7. Molecular mass and Empirical formula mass
8. lons and Polyatomic ions
9. Metals or Non-metals

Ans.

1.

Sodium	Helium
Valency of Sodium is one.	Valency of Helium is zero.

2.

Ozone	Nitrogen
Ozone has atomicity 3.	Nitrogen has atomicity 2.

3.

Oxygen	Carbon
Atomic mass is 16 amu.	Atomic mass is 12 amu.

4.

Ferrous oxide	Ferric oxide
The chemical formula isFeO.	The chemical formula is Fe_2O_3.

5.

Potassium	Phosphorus
Symbol of potassium is K.	Symbol of Phosphrous is P.

6.

Valency	Variable valency
It is the combining capacity of elements. For example, valency of fluorine is one.	Certain elements exhibit more than one valency. For example, Iron (two valency, *i.e.*, 2 and 3).

7.

Molecular mass	Empirical formula mass
It is the sum of atomic masses of the constituent atoms present in one molecule of that substance. For example : Molecular mass of C_2H_2 is 26 u.	It is the sum of atomic masses of various elements present in the empirical formula. For example : C_2H_2, its empirical formula is CH. So, empirical formula mass is 13 u.

8.

Ions	Polyatomic ions
It is a positively or negatively charged atom which is formed by the loss or gain of electrons. For example, Na^+ F^-, Cl^-, etc.	It is a charged species consists of more than one atom. For example, CH_3COO^-, etc.

9.

Metals	Non-metal
They are elements with one, two or three electrons in their outermost shell.	They are elements with five, six or seven electrons in their outermost shell.

Chapter 2. Chemical Change and Reaction

1. Effervescence and Precipitate (Definition)
2. Composition reaction and Decomposition reaction (type of reaction)
3. Displacement reaction and Double displacement reaction (type of reaction)
4. Exothermic reaction and Endothermic reaction **[February, 2020]**
5. Photochemical reaction and Electrochemical reaction
6. Precipitation reaction and neutralisation reaction
7. Positive catalyst and Negative catalyst (Catalytic acitivity)
8. Potassium and Platinum (Reactivity)
9. Promoter and Catalyst (Role in chemical reaction)
10. Respiration and Digestion (Type of reaction)
11. Zinc nitrate and Copper nitrate (by heating) **[February, 2020]**
12. CO_2 and SO_2 (by using a suitable reagent) **[February, 2020]**

Ans.

1.

Effervescence	Precipitate
The formation of gas bubbles in a liquid during a reaction is called effervescence.	The formation of insoluble solid substance in a chemical reaction is called precipitate.

2.

Composition reaction	Decomposition reaction
It is a reaction in which two or more substance combine together to form a compound.	It is the reaction in which a compound splits into two or more simpler substances.

3.

Displacement reaction	Double displacement reaction
It is a chemical reaction in which one part of a molecule is replaced by another element.	It is a chemical reaction in which two reacting moelcules exchange their corresponding ions.

4.

Exothermic reaction	Endothermic reaction
The reaction in which heat is liberated is called exothermic reaction.	The reaction in which heat is absorbed is called endothermic reaction.

5.

Photochemical reaction	Electrochemical reaction
It is the reaction that occurs with absorption of light energy.	It is the reaction that occurs with absorption of electrical energy.

6.

Precipitation reaction	Neutralisation reaction
It is a chemical reaction in which two compounds in their aqueous state react to form an insoluble salt (precipitate) as one of the product.	It is chemical reaction between an acid and a base that forms salt and water.

7.

Positive catalysts	Negative catalysts
They accelerate the rate of the reaction (Manganese dioxide).	They retards the rate of reaction (Phosphoric acid).

8.

Potassium	Platinum
Most reactive metal.	Least reactive metal.

9.

Promoter	Catalyst
Promoters improves the activity of catalyst.	Catalysts fasten the rate of reaction.

10.

Respiration	Digestion
It is an example of exothermic reaction.	It is an example of decomposition reaction.

11.

Zinc nitrate	Copper nitrate
Zinc nitrate is a white solid and converts to a yellow compound (ZnO) on heating, this yellow solid further changes to white colour solid when it cools.	Copper nitrate is blue in colour and give a black compound (CuO) when heated.
$2Zn[NO_3]_2 \longrightarrow 2ZnO + 4NO_2 + O_2$ 2Zn[NO₃]₂: White; 2ZnO: yellow -hot, white - cold; 4NO₂: Nitrogen dioxide	$2Cu[NO_3]_2 \xrightarrow{\varnothing} 2CuO + 4NO_2 + O_2$ 2Cu[NO₃]₂: [blue]; 2CuO: [black]; 4NO₂: Nitrogen dioxide

12.

SO_2	CO_2
Sulphur dioxide (SO_2) turns acidified potassium dichromate paper green.	Carbon dioxide (CO_2) does not react.
$K_2Cr_2O_7(aq) + H_2SO_4(aq) + 3SO_2(g) \longrightarrow Cr_2(SO_4)_3(aq) + K_2SO_4(aq) + H_2O$ Potassium dichromate (Orange) + Sulphuric acid + Carbon dioxide → Chromium sulphate (Green) + Potassium sulphate + water	$K_2Cr_2O_7(aq) + H_2SO_4(aq) + CO_2(g) \longrightarrow$ Potassium dichromate + Sulphuric acid + Carbon dioxide No Reaction

Chapter 3. Water

1. Epsom salt and Quicklime (type of substance)
2. Sodium nitrate and Calcium sulphate dihydrate (Solubility on increasing temperature)
3. Endothermic and Exothermic process (Solubility)
4. Drying agent and Dehydrating agent
5. Hydrated and Anhydrous substance
6. Hard water and Soft water **[February, 2020]**
7. Temporary and Permanent hardness
8. Dilute and Concentrated solution
9. Unsaturated and Saturated solution
10. Efflorescence and Deliquescence **[February, 2020]**

Ans.

1.

Epsom salt	Quick lime
Epsom salt is a efflorescent substance.	Quick lime is a hygroscopic substance.

2.

Sodium nitrate	Calcium sulphate dihyrate
Solubility increase with rise in temperature.	After attaining a certain temperature, solubility decrease with further increases in temperature.

3.

Endothermic process	Exothermic process
In this process, the solubility of the solute increases with increase in temeprature.	In this process, the solubility of the solute increases with lowering in temperature.

4.

Drying agent	Dehydrating agent
They remove moisture content from other substances.	They remove chemically combined elements of water in the ratio of 2 : 1 (hydrogen : oxygen) from a compound.

5.

Hydrated substance	Anhydrous substance
They contain water molecules along with the salts like sodium carbonate decahydrate Example : $Na_2CO_3.10H_2O$.	They do not contain any water along with the salts. Example : NaCl.

6.

Hard water	Soft water
It does not readily form lather with soap.	It readily forms lather with soap.

7.

Temporary hardness	Permanent hardness
Hard water which contains hydrogen carbonates and carbonatesof calcium and magnesium.	Hard water which contains sulphates, nitrates and chlorides of magnesium and calcium.

8.

Dilute solution	Concentrated solution
In this solution, the amount of solute is less as compared to the mass of the solvent.	In this solution, the amount of solute is relatively more for a given mass of the solvent.

9.

Unsaturated solution	Saturated solution
A solution in which more solute can be dissolved at a given temperature.	A solution in which more solute cannot be dissolved at a given temperature.

10.

Efflorescence	Deliquescence
It occurs when vapour pressure in the hydrated crystals exceeds atmospheric vapour pressure.	It occurs when vapour pressure inside the crystal is very low as compared to vapour pressure in the atmospheric pressure.

Chapter 4. Atomic Structure and Chemical Bonding

1. Oxidation and Reduction
2. Magnesium atom and Magnesium ion
3. Covalent bond and Ionic bond
4. Non-metals and Metals
5. Isotope and Isobars
6. Oxidising agent and reducing agent

Ans.

1.

Oxidation	Reduction
The loss of electrons from an atom is called oxidation.	The gain of electrons to an atom is called reduction.
Electropositive atoms undergoes oxidation.	Electronegative atoms undergoes reduction.

2.

Magnesium atom	Magnesium ion
Magnesium atom is represented as Mg.	Magnesium ion is represented as Mg^{2+}.
Electronic configuration of magnesium atom is 2, 8, 2.	Electronic configuration of magnesium ion is 2, 8.

3.

Covalent bond	Ionic bond
The bond formed between two combining atoms by mutual sharing of one or more pair of electrons.	The chemical bond formed as a result of the transfer of electrons from one atom of an element to one atom of another element.
This bond is formed between two non- metals.	This bond is formed between one metal and one non-metal.

4.

Metals	Non-metals
They have one, two or three electrons in their valenced shell. Example, sodium, aluminium, etc.	They have five, six or seven electrons in their valenced shell. Example, oxygen, chlorine, etc.
They undergo oxidation reaction.	They undergo reduction reaction.

5.

Isotopes	Isobars
Isotopes are the atoms of the same possessing different mass number but same atomic number.	They are atoms of different elements with the same mass number but different atomic numbers.
They have same chemical properties.	They have different chemical properties.
Example : Protium, deuterium, tritium (all are isotopes of hydrogen).	Example : $^{40}_{18}Ar$ and $^{40}_{20}Ca$.

6.

Oxidising agent	Reducing agent
The elements which undergo reduction are called oxidising agent.	The elements which undergo oxidation are called reducing agent.

Chapter 5. The Periodic Table

1. Lithium and Sodium (Flame test)
2. Alkali metals and Alkaline earth metals (Valence electron)
3. Inert gas and Halogen (Chemical reactivity)
4. Period 1 and Period 6 (Number of elements)
5. Period and Group (periodic table)
6. Actinides and Lanthanides (atomic number)
7. Period 1 and Period 3 (Number of elements)
8. Mendeleev's Periodic Law and Modern Periodic Law
9. Alkali metals and Inert gas (Reactivity)
10. Sodium and Potassium (Flame test)

Ans.

1.

Lithium	Sodium
Lithium imparts crimson red colour to the flame.	Sodium imparts golden yellow colour to the flame.

2.

Alkali metals	Alkaline earth metals
They have one valence electron.	They have two valence electrons.

3.

Inert gas	Halogen
They are chemically inactive because of stable configuration.	They are very reactive because of incomplete valence shell.

4.

Period 1	Period 6
It is the shortest period (only two elements).	It is the longest period (32 element).

5.

Period	Group
In periodic table, horizontal rows are called period.	In periodic table, vertical columns are called group.

6.

Actinides	Lanthanides
Actinides are the elements of group III B of the seventh period with atomic numbers 89 to 103.	Lanthanides are the elements of group III B of the sixth period with atomic numbers 57 to 71.

7.

Period 1	Period 3
It is the shortest period (Only two elements).	It is the short period (8 element).

8.

Mendeleev's Periodic Law	Modern Periodic Law
According to this law, physical and chemical properties of elements are a periodic function of their atomic masses.	According to this law, physical and chemical properties of elements are a periodic function of their atomic numbers.

9.

Alkali metals	Inert gas
They are very reactive.	They are chemically inert and hence least reactive.

10.

Sodium	Potassium
Sodium burns with golden yellow flame.	Potassium burns with lilac coloured flame.

Chapter 6. Hydrogen

1. Oxidation and Reduction (electrons)
2. Oxidizing agent and Reducing Agent (Hydrogen)

Ans.

1.

Oxidation	Reduction
Oxidation involves loss of electrons.	Reduction involves gain of electrons.

2.

Oxidising agent	Reducing agent
Hydrogen oxidises other substances by accepting electrons from metals. For example; oxygen, chlorine, etc.	Hydrogen reduces the other substances by providing electrons from non-metal For example; hydrogen sulphide, ammonia, etc.

Chapter 7. Study of Gas Laws

1. Charles's law and Boyle's law

Ans.

1.

Charles' law	Boyle's law
Volume of a given mass of a dry gas is directly proportional to its absolute temperature, if pressure is constant.	Volume of a given mass of a dry gas is inversely proportional to its pressure at constant temperature.

❑

Balancing and Writing Chemical Equations

Set 10

Chapter 1. Language of Chemistry

1. Write balanced chemical equation for the following word reaction.
   (a) Reaction of iron and sulphuric acid
   (b) Reaction of potassium bicarbonate with sulphuric acid
   (c) Potassium dichormate reacts with hydrochloric acid
2. Balance the following reactions.
   (a) $MnO_2 + HCl \rightarrow MnCl_2 + H_2O + Cl_2$
   (b) $Zn + KOH \rightarrow K_2ZnO_2 + H_2$
   (c) $Fe + H_2O \rightarrow Fe_3O_4 + H_2$
3. Balance the following equations : **[February, 2020]**
   (a) $P + O_2 \rightarrow P_2O_5$
   (b) $C_2H_4 + O_2 \rightarrow CO_2 + H_2O$
   (c) $P_2O_5 + H_2O \rightarrow H_3PO_4$
4. Write a balanced chemical equation for the following word equations : **[November, 2019]**
   (a) Iron + Chlorine → Iron (III) chloride
   (b) Potassium Chlorate → Potassium chloride + Oxygen
   (c) Potassium Iodide + Nitrogen dioxide → Potassium nitrate + Iodine + Nitric oxide.
5. Write product and balance the following.
   (a) $H_2O + Cl_2 \rightarrow$
   (b) $Na + H_2O \rightarrow$
   (c) $CaO + CO_2 \rightarrow$
   (d) $Mg + H_2SO_4 \rightarrow$

Ans.

1. (a) $Fe + H_2SO_4 \rightarrow FeSO_4 + H_2$
   (b) $2KHCO_3 + H_2SO_4 \rightarrow K_2SO_4 + 2CO_2 + 2H_2O$
   (c) $K_2Cr_2O_7 + 14HCl \rightarrow 2KCl + 2CrCl_3 + 7H_2O + 3Cl_2$
2. (a) $MnO_2 + 4HCl \rightarrow MnCl_2 + 2H_2O + Cl_2$
   (b) $Zn + 2KOH \rightarrow K_2ZnO_2 + H_2$
   (c) $3Fe + 4H_2O \rightarrow Fe_3O_4 + 4H_2$
3. (a) $4P + 5O_2 \rightarrow 2P_2O_5$
   (b) $C_2H_4 + 3O_2 \rightarrow 2CO_2 + 2H_2O$
   (c) $P_2O_5 + 3H_2O \rightarrow 2H_3PO_4$
4. (a) $2\ Fe + 3\ Cl_2 \rightarrow 2\ FeCl_3$
   (b) $2\ KClO_3 \rightarrow 2\ KCl + 3O_2$
   (c) $2\ KI + 4\ NO_2 \rightarrow 2KNO_3 + I_2 + 2\ NO$

5. (a) $2H_2O + Cl_2 \rightarrow 4HCl + O_2$
   (b) $Na + H_2O \rightarrow 2NaOH + H_2$
   (c) $CaO + CO_2 \rightarrow CaCO_3$
   (d) $Mg + H_2SO_4 \rightarrow MgSO_4 + H_2$

Chapter 2. Chemical Change and Reaction

1. Write chemical reactions and balance the following :
   (a) Reaction of sodium hydroxide and hydrochloric acid.
   (b) Zinc reacts with dilute sulphuric acid
   (c) Silver nitrate solution is added to sodium chloride solution.
   (d) Action of dilute sulphuric acid on potassium hydroxide. [November, 2019]
   (e) Reaction of iron and copper sulphate solution. [November, 2019]
2. Balance the following reaction.
   (a) $H_2O_2 \rightarrow H_2O + O_2$
   (b) $PbO + HNO_3 \rightarrow Pb(NO_3)_2 + H_2O$
   (c) $Cl_2 + KBr \rightarrow KCl + Br_2$
3. Write the products of the following chemical reaction and also balance them.
   (a) $Pb\ (NO_3)_2 + KI \rightarrow$
   (b) $NH_3 + O_2 \xrightarrow{Pt}$
   (c) $ZnCO_3 \xrightarrow{\Delta}$
   (d) $H_2SO_4 + 2NaOH \rightarrow$
4. Complete the following chemical equations :
   (a) $Cu(NO_3)_2 + NaOH \longrightarrow$
   (b) $Pb(NO_3)_2 + HCl \longrightarrow$
   (c) $Pb(NO_3)_2 + Na_2CO_3 \longrightarrow$
   (d) $Pb(NO_3)_2 + Na_2SO_4 \longrightarrow$
   (e) $BaCl_2 + Na_2SO_4 \longrightarrow$
   (f) $FeCl_2 + NaOH \longrightarrow$
   (g) $FeCl_3 + NaOH \longrightarrow$
   (h) $MgSO_4 + NaOH \longrightarrow$
   (i) $Ca(NO_3)_2 \xrightarrow{\Delta}$
   (j) $AgNO_3 \xrightarrow{\Delta}$
   (k) $Cu(OH)_2 \xrightarrow{\Delta}$
   (l) $Pb_3O_4 \xrightarrow{\Delta}$
   (m) $Ag_2O \xrightarrow{\Delta}$
   (n) $Pb(NO_3)_2 + NaCl \longrightarrow$
   (o) $PCl_5 \underset{cool}{\overset{\Delta}{\rightleftharpoons}}$
   (p) $HgO \xrightarrow{\Delta}$
   (q) $PbO_3 \xrightarrow{\Delta}$

(r) $KNO_3 \xrightarrow{\Delta}$

(s) $NaNO_3 \xrightarrow{\Delta}$

Ans.

1.

(a) $NaOH + HCl \rightarrow NaCl + H_2O$

(b) $Zn + H_2SO_4 \rightarrow ZnSO_4 + H_2$

(c) $AgNO_3 + NaCl \rightarrow AgCl + NaNO_3$

(d) $2KOH(aq) + H_2SO_4\,(aq) \rightarrow K_2SO_4\,(aq) + 2H_2O\,(l)$

(e) $Fe(s) + CuSO_4\,(aq) \rightarrow FeSO_4\,(aq) + Cu(s)$

2.

(a) $2H_2O_2 \rightarrow 2H_2O + O_2$

(b) $PbO + 2HNO_3 \rightarrow Pb(NO_3)_2 + H_2O$

(c) $Cl_2 + 2KBr \rightarrow 2KCl + Br_2$

3.

(a) $Pb(NO_3)_2 + 2KI \rightarrow 2KNO_3 + PbI_2$

(b) $4NH_3 + 5O_2 \xrightarrow{Pt} 4NO + 6H_2O$

(c) $ZnCO_3 \xrightarrow{\varnothing} ZnO + CO_2$

(d) $H_2SO_4 + 2NaOH \rightarrow Na_2SO_4 + 2H_2O$

4. (a) $Cu(NO_3)_2 + 2NaOH \longrightarrow Cu(OH)_2 + 2NaNO_3$

(b) $Pb(NO_3)_2 + 2HCl \longrightarrow PbCl_2 + 2HNO_3$

(c) $Pb(NO_3)_2 + Na_2SO_4 \longrightarrow PbCO_3 + 2NaNO_3$

(d) $Pb(NO_3)_2 + Na_2SO_4 \longrightarrow PbSO_4 + 2NaNO_3$

(e) $BaCl_2 + Na_2SO_4 \longrightarrow BaSO_4 + 2NaCl$

(f) $FeCl_2 + 2\,NaOH \longrightarrow Fe(OH)_2 + 2NaCl$

(g) $FeCl_3 + 3NaOH \longrightarrow Fe(OH)_3 + 3NaCl$

(h) $MgSO_4 + 2NaOH \longrightarrow Mg(OH)_2 + Na_2SO_4$

(i) $2Ca(NO_3) \xrightarrow{\Delta} 2CaO + 4NO_2\,m + O_2$

(j) $2AgNO_3 \xrightarrow{\Delta} 2Ag + 2\,NO_2 + O_2$

(k) $Cu(OH)_2 \xrightarrow{\Delta} CuO + H_2O$

(l) $2Pb_3\,O_4 \xrightarrow{\Delta} 6PbO + O_2$

(m) $2Ag_2O \xrightarrow{\Delta} 4Ag + O_2$

(n) $Pb(NO_3)_2 + 2NaCl \xrightarrow{\Delta} PbCl_2 + 2NaNO_3$.

(o) $PCl_5 \underset{cool}{\overset{\Delta}{\rightleftharpoons}} PCl_3 + Cl_2$

(p) $2HgO \xrightarrow{\Delta} 2Hg + O_2$

(q) $2PbO_2 \xrightarrow{\Delta} 2PbO + O_2$

(r) $2KNO_3 \xrightarrow{\Delta} 2KNO_2 + O_2$

(s) $2NaNO_3 \xrightarrow{\Delta} 2NaNO_2 + O_2$

Chapter 3. Water

1. Balance the following chemical equations : **[November, 2019]**
   (a) $PbO + NH_3 \rightarrow Pb + H_2O + N_2$
   (b) $C_2H_5OH + O_2 \rightarrow CO_2 + H_2O$
   (c) $Fe + O_2 \rightarrow Fe_3O_4$
2. Write a balanced chemical equation for each of the following : **[February, 2020]**
   (a) Action of heat on calcium bicarbonate
   (b) Action of dilute sulphuric acid on sodium carbonate
   (c) Action of hot water on heated magnesium
   (d) Action of dilute hydrochloric acid on iron.
   (e) Action of sodium hydroxide solution on aluminium.

Ans.

1. (a) $3\,PbO + 2\,NH_3 \rightarrow 3\,Pb + 3\,H_2O + N_2$
   (b) $C_2H_5OH + 3O_2 \rightarrow 2\,CO_2 + 3\,H_2O$
   (c) $3\,Fe + 2\,O_2 \rightarrow Fe_3O_4$
2. (a) $CaHCO_3 \xrightarrow{Heat} CaCO_3 + CO_2 + H_2O$
   Calcium bicarbonate, Calcium carbonate, Carbon dioxide, water
   (b) $H_2SO_{4(aq)} + Na_2CO_{3(aq)} \longrightarrow H_2O_{(i)} + CO_{2(g)} + Na_2SO_{4(aq)}$
   Dil-sulphuric acid, Sodium carbonate, Water, Carbon dioxide, Sodium sulphate
   (c) $Mg\,(s) + H_2O(g) \longrightarrow MgO\,(s) + H_2(g)$
   Magnesium, Steam, Magnesium oxide + Hydrogen gas
   (d) $2\,Fe(s) + 6\,HCl(aq) \longrightarrow 2\,FeCl_3(aq) + 3\,H_2(g)$
   Iron, Dil.hydrochloric acid, Ferric chloride, Hydrogen
   (e) $2\,Al + 3NaOH \longrightarrow Al(OH)_3 \downarrow + 3\,Na^+$
   Aluminium, Sodium hydroxide, White ppt.
   $Al(OH)_3 + NaOH \longrightarrow Na^+[Al(OH)_4]^-$
   Sodium tetrahydroxoaluminate (III) (Soluble complex)

Chapter 6. Hydrogen

1. Write balanced chemical equations for each of the following :
   (a) Iron reacts with dil. HCl.
   (b) Action of sodium hydroxide solution on zinc. **[November, 2019]**
   (c) Lead reacts with potassium hydroxide.
   (d) Aluminium reacts with fused sodium hydroxide.
   (e) Reaction of nitrogen and hydrogen. **[November, 2019]**
2. Write balanced equations and give your observations when the following metals react :
   (a) Action of cold water on sodium. **[November, 2019]**
   (b) Calcium with cold water.
   (c) Magnesium with boiling water.
   (d) Magnesium with steam.

3. Give equations to express the reaction between :
   (a) Steam and red hot iron.
   (b) Calcium and water.
4. Complete and balance the following reaction.
   (a) $Zn + HCl \rightarrow$
   (b) $Al + H_2SO_4 \rightarrow$
   (c) $Al + NaOH + H_2O \longrightarrow$ ________ + ________
   (d) $N_2 + H_2 \longrightarrow$ ________
   (e) $Fe + H_2SO_4 \longrightarrow$ ________ + ________
   (f) $CaH_2 + H_2O \longrightarrow$ ________ + ________
   (g) $Fe + HCl \longrightarrow$ ________ + ________
   (h) $CuO + H_2 \longrightarrow$ ________ + ________
   (i) $Na + H_2O \longrightarrow$ ________ + ________
   (j) $Fe + H_2O \rightleftharpoons$ ________ + ________
   (k) $H_2S + Cl_2 \longrightarrow$ ________ + ________
   (l) $Zn + H_2O \longrightarrow$ ________ + ________
   (m) $Al + H_2O \longrightarrow$ ________ + ________
   (n) $Pb + NaOH \longrightarrow$ ________ + ________
   (o) $Mg + \underset{\text{Steam}}{H_2O} \longrightarrow$ ________ + ________
   (p) $Mg + HNO_3 \longrightarrow$ ________ + ________
   (q) $Mg + HCl \longrightarrow$ ________ + ________
   (r) $Mg + H_2SO_4 \longrightarrow$ ________ + ________

Ans.

1. (a) $Fe + 2HCl \rightarrow FeCl_2 + H_2$
   (b) $Zn + 2NaOH \rightarrow \underbrace{Na_2ZnO_2}_{\text{Sodium zincate}} + H_2$
   (c) $Pb + 2KOH \rightarrow K_2PbO_2 + H_2$
   (d) $2Al + \underbrace{6NaOH}_{\text{Fused}} \longrightarrow \underbrace{2Na_3AlO_3}_{\text{Sodium aluminate}} + 3H_2$
   (e) $N_2(g) + 3H_2(g) \rightarrow 2NH_3(g)$
2. (a) When sodium reacts with cold water sodium hydroxide is formed. The reaction is less vigorous and less exothermic than potassium. Bubbles of hydrogen gas are produced and the solution formed is colourless, soapy, slightly warm and alkaline.

$$2Na + 2H_2O \rightarrow 2NaOH + H_2.$$

   (b) When calcium reacts with water, bubbles of hydrogen are liberated and the solution turns milky, turbid and alkaline.

$$Ca + 2H_2O \rightarrow Ca(OH)_2$$

   (c) Magnesium reacts slowly with boiling water and forms a base, magnesium hydroxide liberating hydrogen gas.

$$Mg + 2H_2O \rightarrow Mg(OH)_2 + H_2\uparrow$$

(d) Magnesium burns in steam with an intense white light, liberating hydrogen gas and white ash, that is magnesium oxide.

$$Mg + H_2O \rightarrow MgO + H_2 \uparrow$$

3. (a) $3Fe + 4H_2O \rightarrow Fe_3O_4 + 4H_2\uparrow$

(b) $Ca + 2H_2O \rightarrow Ca(OH)_2 + H_2$

4. (a) $Zn + 2HCl \rightarrow ZnCl_2 + H_2$

(b) $2Al + 3H_2SO_4 \rightarrow Al_2(SO_4)_3 + 3H_2$

(c) $2Al + 2NaOH + 2H_2O \longrightarrow 2NaAlO_2 + 3H_2$

(d) $N_2 + 3H_2 \longrightarrow 2NH_3$

(e) $Fe + H_2SO_4 \longrightarrow FeSO_4 + H_2$

(f) $CaH_2 + 2H_2O \longrightarrow Ca\ (OH)_2 + 2H_2$

(g) $Fe + 2HCl \longrightarrow FeCl_2 + H_2$

(h) $CuO + H_2 \longrightarrow Cu + H_2O$

(i) $2Na + 2H_2O \longrightarrow 2\ NaOH + H_2$

(j) $3Fe + 4H_2O \rightleftharpoons Fe_3\ O_4 + 4H_2$

(k) $H_2S + Cl_2 \longrightarrow 2HCl + S$

(l) $Zn + H_2O \longrightarrow ZnO + H_2$

(m) $2Al + 3H_2O \longrightarrow Al_2O_3 + 3H_2$

(n) $Pb + 2NaOH \longrightarrow Na_2PbO_2 + H_2$

(o) $Mg + H_2O \longrightarrow MgO + H_2$
Steam

(p) $Mg + 2HNO_3 \longrightarrow Mg(NO_3)_2 + H_2$

(q) $Mg + 2HCl \longrightarrow MgCl_2 + H_2$

(r) $Mg + H_2SO_4 \longrightarrow MgSO_4 + H_2$

❑

Chemical Naming and Formulation

| Set 11 |

Chapter 1. Language of Chemistry

1. Write the chemical formula of the following compounds.
   (a) Magnesium chloride (b) Ammonium hydroxide (c) Calcium hydrogen sulphite
   (d) Bromine molecule (e) Ammonium dichromate (f) Sulphite radical
   (g) Ammonium ion

Ans.

(a) $MgCl_2$ (b) NH_4OH (c) $Ca(HSO_3)_2$
(d) Br_2 (e) $(NH_4)_2 Cr_2O_7$
(f) SO_3^- (g) NH_4^+

2. Write the chemical name of the following compounds.
   (a) $CaSiO_3$ (b) Mg_3N_2 (c) $CuCl_2$
   (d) $KMnO_4$

Ans.

(a) Calcium silicate (b) Magnesium nitride (c) Cupric chloride
(d) Potassium permanganate

3. Formulate the following compounds:
   (a) Calcium oxide (b) Sodium aluminate (c) Aluminum hydroxide

Ans.

Name of compound	Symbols with valencies and charge	Exchange of valency	Formula
(a) Calcium oxide	Ca^{2+} O^{2-} (Dividing by HCF it becomes Ca^+ O^-)	Ca^{+2} O^2 → Ca_1 O_1	CaO (Cancelling the common factor)
(b) Sodium aluminate	Na^+ AlO_2^-	Na^1 AlO_2^- → Na_1 $(AlO_2)_1$	$NaAlO_2$
(c) Aluminium hydroxide	Al^{3+} OH^-	Al^{3+} OH^1 → Al_1 $(OH)_3$	$Al(OH)_3$

4. The formula of the chloride of a metal M is MCI. Write the formula of its: **[February, 2020]**
   (a) Sulphate
   (b) Zincate
   (c) Hydroxide

Ans. (a) M_2SO_4

(b) M_2ZnO_2

(c) MOH

5. Give the formulae of: **[February, 2020]**

(a) Sodium bisulphate

(b) Ammonium nitrate

(c) Magnesium nitride

Ans. (a) $NaHSO_4$

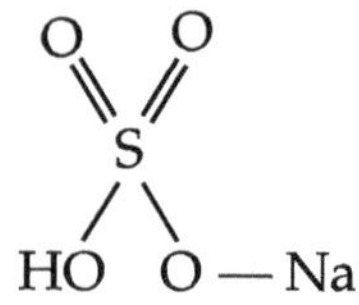

(b) NH_4NO_3

(c) Mg_3N_2

Chapter 3. Water

Write the chemical formula of the following substances: **[November, 2019]**

(a) Caustic potash (b) Quick lime (c) Blue Vitriol

Ans.

(a) KOH (b) CaO (c) $CuSO_4$

Chapter 4. Atomic Structure and Chemical Bonding

1. Draw the orbital diagram of:

(a) Oxygen

(b) Ammonia molecule

(c) Water molecule **[November, 2019]**

(d) Magnesium chloride **[November, 2019]**

(e) Chlorine molecule **[November, 2019]**

(f) Hydrogen sulphide

Ans.

(a) Orbital structure of O_2:

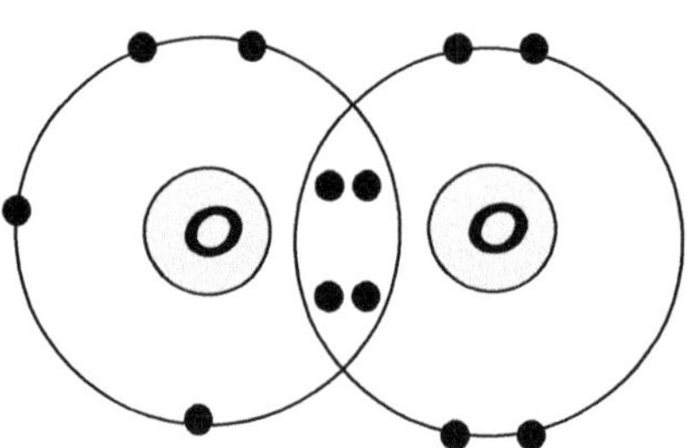

Oxygen molecule

(b) Orbital structure of NH_3:

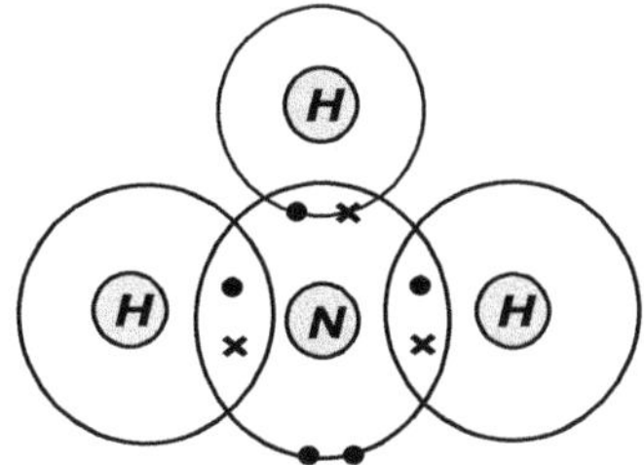

Ammonia molecule

(c) Orbital structure of H_2O:

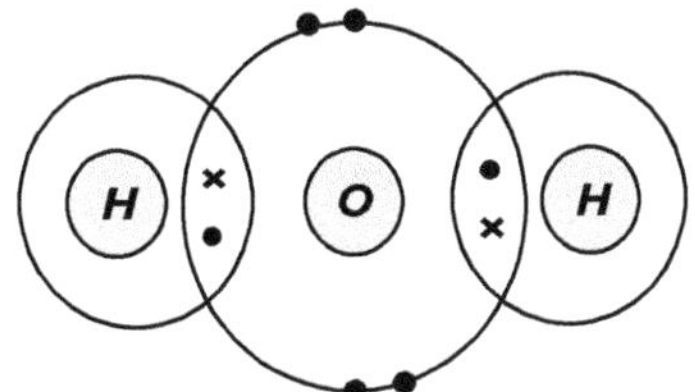

Water molecule

(d) Orbital structure of $MgCl_2$:

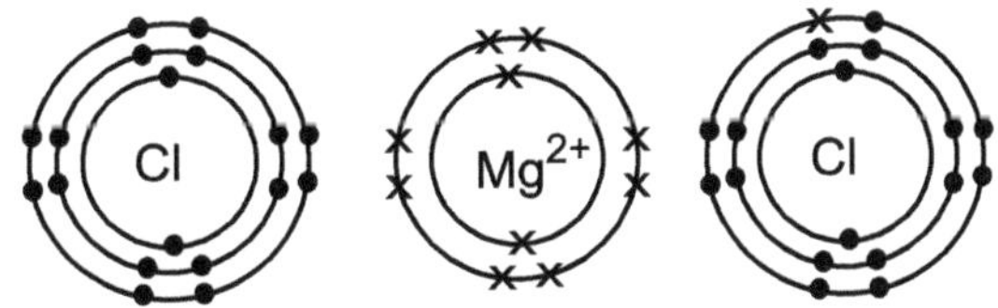

(e) Orbital structure of Cl_2:

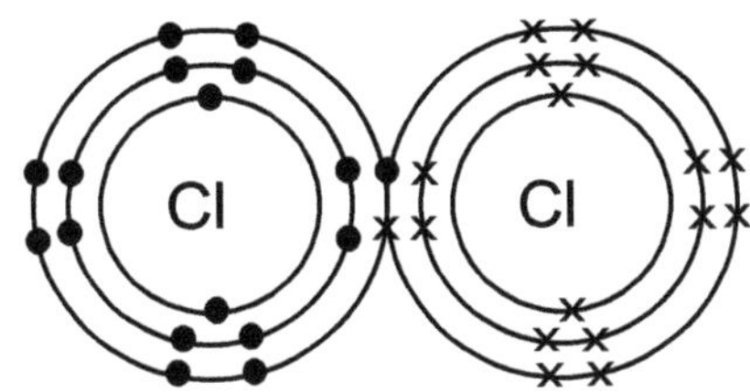

(f) Orbital structure of Hydrogen Sulphide (H_2S):

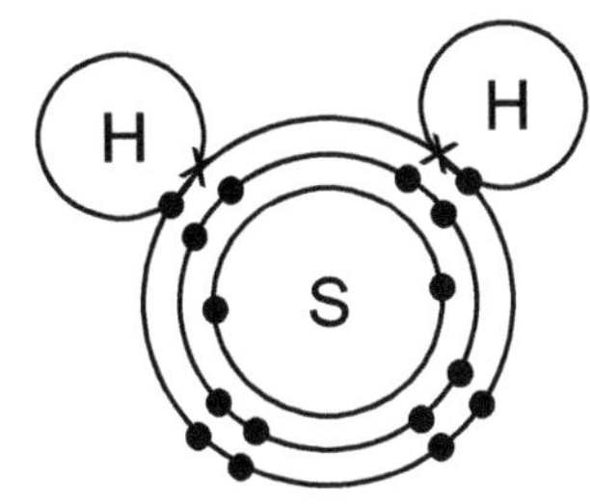

2. Draw the orbit structure to show the formation of the following: **[February, 2020]**

(a) Oxygen molecule

(b) Ammonia

(c) Calcium oxide

Ans. (a) Orbit structure for oxygen molecule (O_2):

Atomic no. of oxygen = 8

Electronic configuration 8 = 2, 6

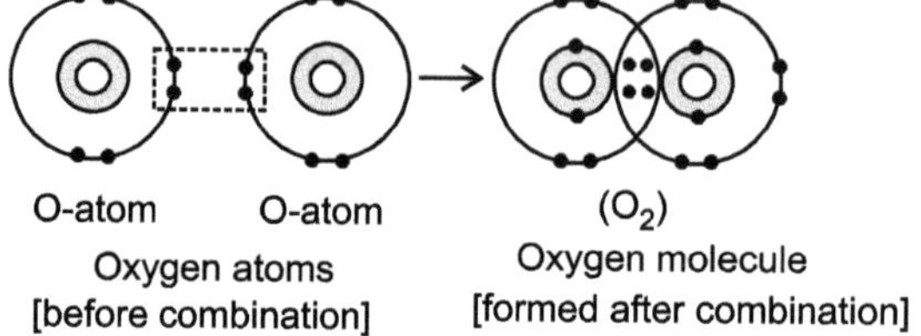

(b) Orbit structure for ammonia molecule (NH_3):

Atomic number of N = 7

Electronic configuration of N = 2, 5

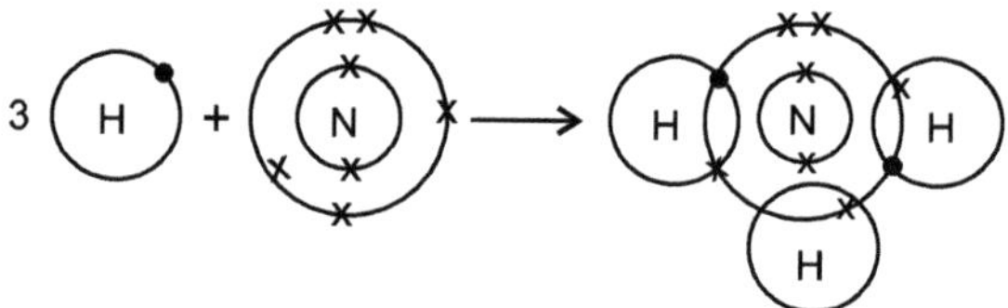

(c) Orbit structure for calcium oxide (CaO):

Atomic number of Ca = 20

Electronic configuration of Ca = 2, 8, 8, 2

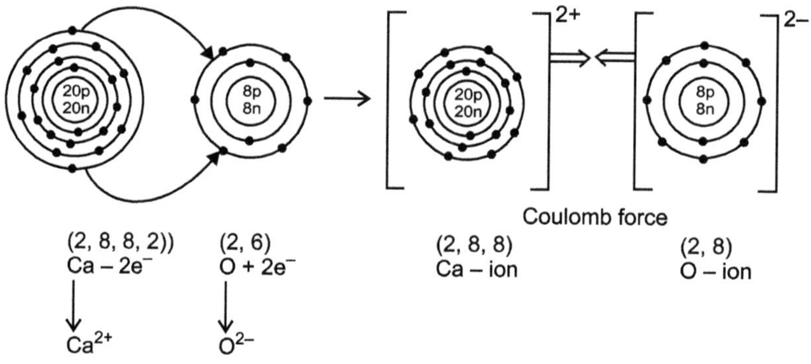

❑

Define the Following

Set 12

Define the following:

Chapter 1. Language of Chemistry

1. Element
2. Atom
3. Atomicity
4. Molecule
5. Valency
6. Ion
7. Radical
8. Chemical equation
9. Empirical formula
10. Atomic mass unit

Ans.

1. An element is a simple and pure form of matter which cannot be decomposed into simpler substances.
2. An atom is the smallest particle of an element which may or may not exist independently but can take part in a chemical reaction.
3. The number of atoms in a molecule of an element is called its atomicity.
4. A molecule is the smallest particle that has the capability to exist independently.
5. The number of valenced electrons that an atom can lose, gain or share during a chemical reaction is called valency.
6. An ion is a positively or negatively charged atom which is formed by loss or gain of electrons by an atom or group of atoms.
7. A radical is an atom or group of atoms of the same or of different elements that behaves as a single unit with a positive or negative charge.
8. A chemical equation is the symbolic representation of a chemical reaction using the symbols and formulae of the substances involved in the reaction.
9. The empirical formula of a compound is the simplest formula, which gives the simplest ratio in whole number of atoms of different elements present in one molecule of the compound.
10. Atomic mass unit is equal to one twelfth the mass of an atom of carbon-12.

Chapter 2. Chemical Change and Reaction

1. Thermal decomposition
2. Inhibitors
3. Catalyst **[November, 2019]**
4. Positive catalyst
5. Promoters
6. Chemical change
7. Chemical bond
8. Combination reaction
9. Displacement reaction
10. Decomposition reaction
11. Double displacement reaction

Ans.

1. A decomposition reaction that is brought about by heat without any recombination on cooling is known as thermal decomposition.
2. A calatyst is used to retard a reaction is known as inhibitors or negative catalyst. For example, phosphoric acid.
3. Catalysts are substances which increase the rate of reaction without being used up in the reaction. They provide an alternative mechanism for the reaction which lowers activation energy.
4. When a catalyst accelerates a reaction, that catalyst is known as positive catalyst. For example, iron, manganese oxide, etc.

5. Promoters are the substance which influences the rate of a chemical reaction by improving the efficiency of the catalyst.
6. A chemical change is a permanent change in which the chemical composition of a substance is changed and one or more new substances formed with different chemical compositions and properties.
7. A chemical bond is the force which holds the atoms of a molecule together, as in a compound.
8. A reaction in which two or more substances combine to form a new substance is called a combination reaction.
9. Displacement reaction is a chemical reaction in which one part of a molecule is replaced by highly reactive element.
10. Decomposition reaction is the reaction in which a compound splits into two or more simpler substances.
11. A reaction in which two reacting molecules exchange their corresponding ions is called as double displacement reaction.

Chapter 3. Water

1. Supersaturated solution
2. Concentration of a solution
3. Crystallisation
4. Hygrosocpy
5. Efflorescence
6. Drying agents
7. Mass percent
8. Solubility
9. Binary solution
10. Volume percent
11. Deliquescence

[November, 2019]

Ans.

1. A solution that contains more solute than its saturated solution at a given temperature is called supersaturated solution.
2. Concentration of a solution is defined as the amount of solute dissolve in a given quantity of that solution.
3. Crystallisation is a process in which crystals of a substance are obtained by cooling a hot saturated solution.
4. Hygroscopy is a phenomenon of attracting and holding water molecues via absorption.
5. Efflorescence is a phenomenon where a compound loses its water of crystallisation on exosure to dry air.
6. Drying agents are the substances which readily absorb moisture from other substances without chemically reacting with them.
7. Mass percent is defined as the mass of solid solute in grams present in 100 grams of the solution. It is used when solute is solid and solvent is liquid.
8. Solubility is defined as the amount of solute dissolve in 100g of solvent to form a saturated solution at a particular temperature.
9. A solution which is made up of two compoenent is termed as binary solution.
10. Volume percent is defined as the volume of solute in millilitres present in 100mL of solution. It is used when solute and solvent both are liquids.
11. Deliquescence is the property by virtue of which a solid substance absorbs water from atmosphere and is converted ito a solution. For example, solid soidum hydroxide, magnesium chloride, etc.

Chapter 4. Atomic Structure and Chemical Bonding

1. Atom
2. Mass number
3. Valency
4. Chemical bond
5. Electrovalency
6. Ion
7. Octet rule
8. Ionic bond
9. Covalent molecule
10. Covalency
11. Isotopes **[February, 2020]**
12. Electrovalent bond **[February, 2020]**
13. Atomic number **[February, 2020]**

Ans.

1. An atom is the smallest particle of an element that exhibits all the properites of that element.
2. Mass number of an element is the total number of protons and neutrons present in the nucleus.
3. The number of electrons gained, lost or shared to attain the octet in the outermost shell, gives the combining capacity of the element. That is its valency.
4. A chemical bond is the force of attraction between the two atoms that binds them together as a unit called molecule.
5. The number of electrons that an atom of an element loses or gains to form an electrovalent bond is called electrovalency.
6. An ion is a charged particle which is formed due to the gain or the loss of one or more electrons by an atom.
7. During chemical reactions, atoms of all the elements become stable by acquiring electronic configuration of the nearest inert gas *i.e.*, eight electrons in the outermost orbit, this is known as octet rule.
8. The chemical bonds formed as a result of the transfer of electrons from one atom of an element to one atom of another element are called ionic bonds.
9. The molecule formed due to sharing of electrons is called covalent molecule.
10. The covalency of an atom is the number of its electrons taking part in the formation of shared pairs.
11. Isotopes are atoms of the same element which contain different number of neutrons but same number of protons. Hence, the atomic number and chemical property of any two isotopes of a given element would be same but the mass number would differ.

    For example :

    Mass number (A) $^{63}_{29}Cu$ Protons (Z) = 29

    Atomic number (Z) Neutorons (N) = 34

    $^{65}_{29}Cu$ Protons (Z) = 29

    Neutrons (N) = 36
12. Electrovalent bonds are the strong bonds formed when oppositely charged ions attracted to each other. These are non-directional bonds formed between cations (formed by loss of electron from their valence shell) and anions (formed by gain of electron in their valence shell). For example, NaCl.

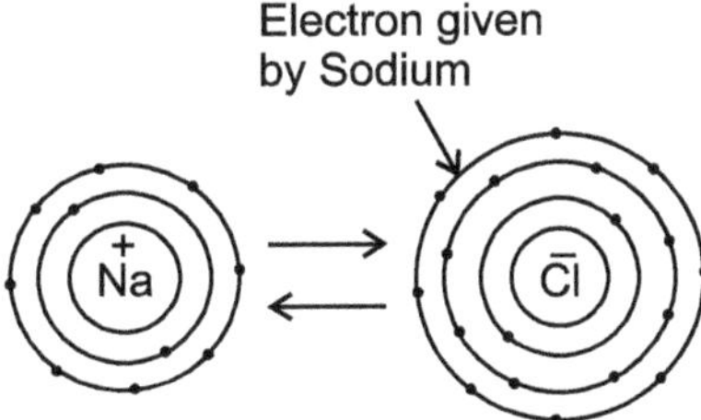

13. The atomic number of any element is given by the number of protons in its nucleus. It defines the particular element. For example, Ag.

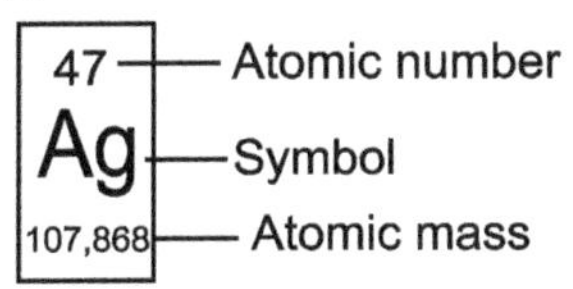

Chapter 5. The Periodic Table

1. Typical elements
2. Newland's law of Octaves
3. Periods in the periodic table
4. Inert gas
5. Bridge elements
6. Periodic properties

Ans.

1. The third period elements, Na, Mg, Al, Si, P, S and Cl summarise the properties of their respective groups and are typical elements.

2. According to Newland's law of octaves, when elements are arranged by increasing atomic mass, the properties of every eighth element starting from any element are repetition of the periodic properties of the starting element.
3. There are seven horizontal rows in the modern periodic table, each called as a period.
4. Elements of zero group, which is the 18th vertical column are known as inert gases or noble gases.
5. Elements of second period show resemblance in properties with elements of the next group of the third period, leading to a diagonal relationship. Such elements are called bridge elements.
6. Properties that reappear at regular intervals or in which there is gradual variation, *i.e.,* increase or decrease at regular intervals, are called periodic properties.

Chapter 6. Hydrogen

1. Oxidation
2. Reduction
3. Redox reaction
4. Oxidising agent
5. Reducing agent
6. Hydrogenation
7. Activity series of metals

Ans.

1. Oxidation is defined as a process in which an atom or ion loses electron.
2. Reduction is defined as a process in which an atom or ion gains electrons.
3. A reaction in which oxidation and reduction takes place simultaneously is called redox reaction
4. An oxidising agent is a substance which transfers oxygen to another substance, or removes hydrogen from that substance.
5. A reducing agent is a substance which transfers hydrogen to another substance, or removes oxygen from that substance.
6. In the presence of a catalyst like nickel, hydrogen directly combines with organic compounds that have double or triple bonds between two carbon atoms. This process is known as hydrogenation.
7. Arrangement of metals in decreasing order of reactivity in the form of a series is called activity series of metals.

Chapter 7. Study of Gas laws

1. S.T. P. and N.T.P.
2. Atmospheric pressure
3. Boyle's law.
4. Charle's law
5. Absolute zero **[November, 2019]**
6. Absolute scale of temperature
7. Ideal gas equation

Ans.

1. The pressure of the atmosphere which is equal to 75 cm or 760 mm of mercury and temperature is 0°C or 273 K is termed as STP (Stantdard temperature and pressure) or NTP (Normal temperature and pressure). Standard temperature = 0°C = 273 K

   Standard pressure = 760 mm Hg = 76 cm Hg = 1atm
2. Our planet is surrounded by a thick blanket of air known as atmosphere. The pressure exerted by air on the surface of earth is called atmospheric pressure.
3. According to Boyle's law, volume of a dry gas is inversely proportional to its pressure at constant temperature.
4. According to Charles' law, the volume of a given mass of a dry gas increases or decreases by 1/273 of its volume at 0°C for each 1°C increase or decrease in temperature respectively if the pressure remains constant.
5. The temperature at which molecular motion completely ceases on the Kelvin scale. –273°C is the absolute zero temperature.

$$V = V_0\left(\frac{273+t}{273}\right)$$

$$\text{Volume at } -273°C = V_0\left(\frac{273-273}{273}\right) = 0$$

6. The temperature scale with zero at –273°C and each degree is equal to each degree on the Celsius scale is termed as absolute scale of temperature.
7. A mathematical expression describing the simultaneous effect of changes in temperature and pressure on volume of a given mass of gas is called the ideal gas equation.

Chapter 8. Atmospheric Pollution

1. Smog
2. Greenhouse effect
3. Global warming
4. Green house gases
5. Acid rain
6. Environmental pollution
7. Pollutant
8. Air pollution
9. Ozone

Ans.

1. Smog is a pollutant which is a combination of oxides of nitrogen and sulphur and of partially oxidised hydrocarbons and their derivatives produced by industries and automobiles forms a dark, thick, dust and soot laden fog.
2. Heating of the earth and its environment due to radiations of the sun trapped by carbon dioxide and water vapor in the atmosphere is called greenhouse effect.
3. On increasing the proportion of green house gases earth's surface temperature will also rise. Rise in average temperature of the earth's surface is called global warming.
4. Gases that contribute to greenhouse effect are carbon dioxide, water vapour, oxides of nitrogen, methane, ozone, chloro-fluoro-carbon, etc., and are thus called green house gases.
5. The term acid rain is used to decribe all precipitations-rain, snow, fog, dew which are more acidic than normal water. Normal rain is only slightly acidic having pH about 5.6 because carbon dioxide reacts with it to form weak carbonic acid.
6. Environmental pollution is the effect of undesirable changes in our surroundings that have a harmful effect on plants, animals and human beings .
7. Toxic and otherwise harmful substances that have an undesirable impact on different components of the environment and life forms are known as pollutants.
8. Air pollination means degradation of air quality due to concentration of harmful contaminants that affects human plant and animal lives.
9. Ozone is a light bluish gas found in the upper layer of atmosphere. Ozone is formed by the action of ultravioilet rays of the sun on oxygen.

❑

Figure and Table Based Questions

Set 13

Chapter 1. Language of Chemistry

1. Complete the following table by writing formula using basic and acidic radicals.

Acid radical → Basic radical ↓	Nitrite	Bicarbonate
Potassium		
Magnesium		

Ans.

Acid radical → Basic radical ↓	Nitrite	Bicarbonate
Potassium	KNO_2	$KHCO_3$
Magnesium	$Mg(NO_2)_2$	$Mg(HCO_3)_2$

2. Complete the following table:

Acid radical→ Basic radical↓	Chloride	Nitrate	Sulphate	Carbonate	Hydroxide	Phosphate
Magnesium						
Sodium						
Zinc						
Silver						
Ammonium						
Calcium						
Iron (II)						
Potassium						

Ans.

Acid radical→ Basic radical↓	Chloride	Nitrate	Sulphate	Carbonate	Hydroxide	Phosphate
Magnesium	$MgCl_2$	$Mg(NO_3)_2$	$MgSO_4$	$MgCO_3$	$Mg(OH)_2$	$Mg_3(PO_4)_2$
Sodium	$NaCl$	$NaNO_3$	Na_2SO_4	Na_2CO_3	$NaOH$	Na_3PO_4
Zinc	$ZnCl_2$	$Zn(NO_3)_2$	$ZnSO_4$	$ZnCO_3$	$Zn(OH)_2$	$Zn_3(PO)_2$
Silver	$AgCl$	$AgNO_3$	Ag_2SO_4	Ag_2CO_3	$AgOH$	Ag_3PO_4

Ammonium	NH_4Cl	NH_4NO_3	$(NH_4)_2SO_4$	$(NH_4)_2CO_3$	NH_4OH	$(NH_4)_3PO_4$
Calcium	$CaCl_2$	$Ca(NO_3)_2$	$CaSO_4$	$CaCO_3$	$Ca(OH)_2$	$Ca_3(PO_4)_2$
Iron (II)	$FeCl_2$	$Fe(NO_3)_2$	$FeSO_4$	$FeCO_3$	$Fe(OH)_2$	$Fe_3(PO_4)_2$
Potassium	KCl	KNO_3	K_2SO_4	K_2CO_3	KOH	K_3PO_4

Chapter 2. Chemical Change and Reaction

1. Complete the table which relates the action of acids on salts.

Salt reacting with acids	Gas evolved	Confirmatory test for gas
Zinc sulphide	(i)	(ii)
Sodium bicarbonate	(iii)	(iv)

Ans. The reaction of Zinc sulphide with HCl is,

$$ZnS + 2HCl \rightarrow ZnCl_2 + H_2S \uparrow$$

(i) Gas evolved in the reaction is hydrogen sulphide with acid is hydrogen sulphide, *i.e.*, H_2S.

(ii) It turns moist blue litmus red.

The reaction of sodium bicarbonate with acid is as follows:

$$2NaHCO_3 + H_2SO_4 \rightarrow Na_2SO_4 + 2H_2O + 2SO_2 \uparrow$$

(iii) Gas evolved in the reaction of sodium bicarbonate with acid is sulphur dioxide, *i.e.*, SO_2.

(iv) Sulphur dioxide decolourises pink acidified potassium permanganate solution.

$$\underbrace{2KMnO_4 + 2H_2O}_{\text{Pink}} + 5SO_2 \rightarrow \underbrace{K_2SO_4 + 2MnSO_4}_{\text{colourless}} + 2H_2SO_4$$

2. Complete the following table which relates to action of heat on substance. **[February, 2020]**

Substance heated	Gas evolved	Residue colour
Zinc Carbonate		
Ammonium dichromate		

Ans.

Substance heated	Gas evolved	Residue colour
Zinc Carbonate	CO_2	Yellow (hot)
Ammonium dichromate	N_2	Green

3. Complete the table which relates the action of bases on salts.

Salt reacting with base	Salt formed	Gas evolved
$NH_4Cl + Ca(OH)_2$	(i)	(ii)
$NH_4Cl + NaOH$	(iii)	(ii)

Ans. The reaction of ammonium chloride with base is,

$$NH_4Cl + Ca(OH)_2 \rightarrow CaCl_2 + 2H_2O + 2NH_3 \uparrow$$

(i) Salt formed in the reaction is $CaCl_2$.

(ii) Gas evolved in the reaction in ammonia, *i.e.*, NH_3.

The reaction of ammonium chloride with another base is,

$$NH_4Cl + NaOH \rightarrow NaCl + H_2O + NH_2 \uparrow$$

(iii) Salt formed in the reaction is sodium chloride, *i.e.*, NaCl

(iv) Gas evolved in the reaction is ammonia, *i.e.*, NH_3.

4. Complete the following table which relates to the action of acid on salts: **[November, 2019]**

Salt reacting with dilute acid	Gas evolved	Confirmatory test of the gas
Sodium sulphite		
Iron (II) sulphide		

Ans.

Salt reacting with dilute acid	Gas evolved	Confirmatory test of the gas
Sodium sulphite	Sulphur dioxide (SO_2)	Sulphur dioxide gas turns acidified potassium dichromate (VI) solution from orange to green and Chromium is reduced from oxidation state of (VI) to (III).
Iron (II) sulphide	Hydrogen sulphide (H_2S)	Filter paper moistened with lead acetate turns black on exposure to gas. $Pb(CH_3COO)_2 + H_2S \rightarrow 2CH_3COOH + PbS$ (Black lead sulphide)

5. Observe the two test tubes A and B in the diagram given below and answer the following questions.

(i) In which test tube, reaction will take place?

(ii) Name the type of reaction.

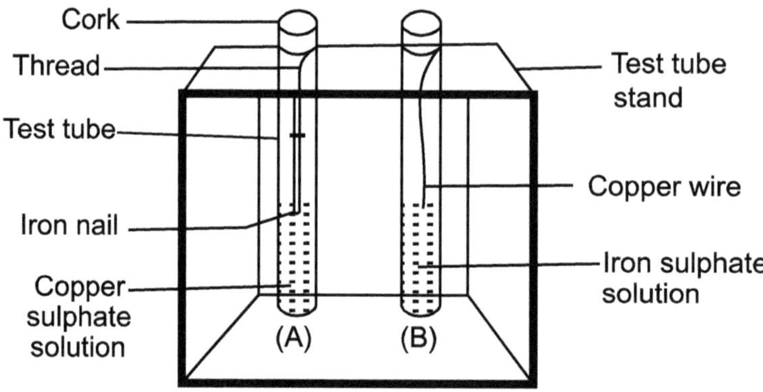

Ans. (i) In test tube, A

(ii) Displacement reaction.

Chapter 3. Water

1. Complete the following table:

Common name	Chemical formula	Efflorescent, hygroscopic or deliquescent substance
Quick lime		
Washing soda		

Ans.

Common name	Chemical formula	Efflorescent, hygroscopic or deliquescent substance
Quick lime	CaO	Hygroscopic substance
Washing soda	$Na_2CO_3.10H_2O$	Efflorescent substance

2. Complete the following table:

Chemical name	Number of water molecules in the compound	Efflorescent, hygroscopic or deliquescent substance
Glauber's salt		
Epsom salt		

Ans.

Chemical name	Number of water molecules in the compound	Efflorescent, hygroscopic or deliquescent substance
Glauber's salt	10 ($Na_2SO_4.10H_2O$)	Effloresncnet substance
Epsom salt	7 ($MgSO_4.7H_2O$)	Efflorescent subsatnce

3. Complete the following table:

Common name	Chemical formula	Acid, base or salt
Solid caustic soda		
Blue vitriol		
Solid caustic potash		

Ans.

Common Name	Chemical formula	Acid, base of salt
Solid caustic soda	NaOH	Base
Blue vitrol	$CuSO_4$	Salt
Solid caustic potash	KOH	Base

4. Identify A, B, C and D.

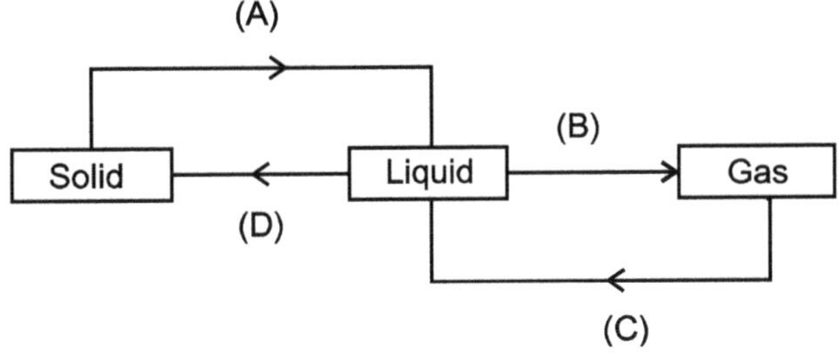

Ans.

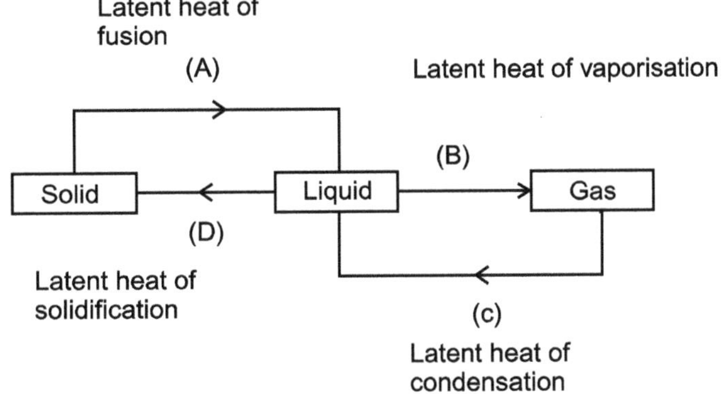

Chapter 4. Atomic Structure and Chemical Bonding

1. In the figure given alongside:

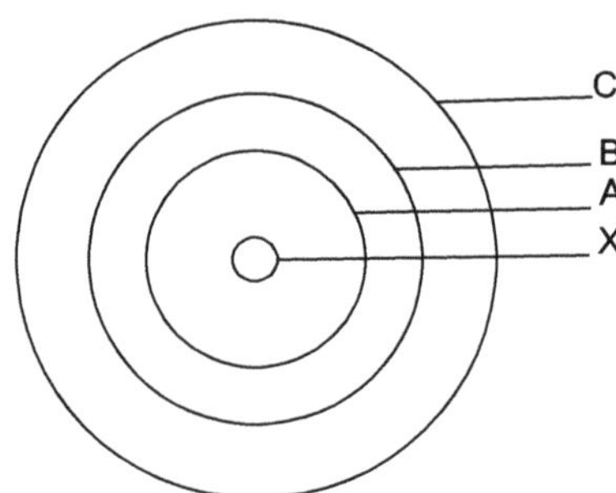

(i) Name the shells denoted by A, B and C. Which shell has least energy?

(ii) Name X and state charge on it.

(iii) The above sketch is of________model of an atom.

Ans.

(i) A denotes K shell, B denotes L shell and C denotes M shell. K shell has least energy.

(ii) X is nucleus and it is positively charged.

(iii) The above sketch is of Bohr's model of an atom

2. Complete the table given below by identifying P, Q, R and S.

Element	Symbol	Number of protons	Number of neutrons	Number of electrons
Sodium	${}^{23}_{11}Na$	11		11
Chlorine	${}^{35}_{17}Cl$		18	17
Uranium		92	146	92
S	${}^{19}_{9}F$	9	10	9

Ans. Number of neutrons = Mass number – Atomic number

Mass number = Atomic number + Number of protons

Element	Symbol	Number of protons	Number of neutrons	Number of electrons
Sodium	${}^{23}_{11}Na$	11	12	11
Chlorine	${}^{35}_{17}Cl$	17	18	17
Uranium	${}^{238}_{92}U$	92	146	92
Fluroine	${}^{19}_{9}F$	9	10	9

3. Complete the following table relating to the atomic structure of some elements.

Element symbol	Atomic number	Mass number	Number of neutrons	Number of electrons	Number of protons
Li	3	6	(i)	(ii)	(iii)
Cl	17	(iv)	20	(v)	(vi)
Na	(vii)	(viii)	12	(ix)	11
Al	(x)	27	(xi)	(xii)	13
S	(xiii)	32	16	(xiv)	(xv)

Ans. For Li, Atomic number = 3 and mass number = 6

Number of neutrons = 6 – 3 = 3

Number of protons and electrons are equal to atomic number.

For Cl, Atomic number = 17 and number of neutrons = 20

Number of protons and electrons are equal to atomic number.

Mas number = 17 + 20 = 37

For Na, Number of protons = 11 and number of neutrons = 12

Atomic number is equal to number of protons.

Mass number = 11 + 12 = 23

For Al, Mass number = 27 and Number of protons = 13

Number of protons and electrons are equal to atomic number

Number of neutrons = 27 – 13 = 14

For S, Mass number = 32 and number of neutrons = 16

Number of protons = 32 – 16 = 16

Number of protons and electrons are equal to atomic number

Element symbol	Atomic number	Mass number	Number of neutrons	Number of electrons	Number of protons
Li	3	6	3	3	3
Cl	17	37	20	17	17
Na	11	23	12	11	11
Al	13	27	14	13	13
S	16	32	16	16	16

4. Complete the following table.

Element	Mass number	Atomic number	Number of protons	Number of electrons	Number of neutrons	Metal or non-metal
Nitrogen	14	7	(i)	(ii)	(iii)	(iv)

Ans. (i) Number of proton is equal to atomic number. So, number of protons in nitrogen atom is 7.

(ii) In an atom, number of proton and number of electron is equal. So, number of electrons in nitrogen atom is 7.

(iii) Mass number = Number of proton + Number of neutron

Number of neutron = 14 – 17 = 7

Hence, number of neutrons in nitrogen atom is 7.

(iv) Electronic configuration of nitrogen atom is 2, 5. As the valence shell consist of five electrons. So, nitrogen is a non-metal.

So, complete table is,

Element	Mass number	Atomic number	Number of protons	Number of electrons	Number of neutrons	Metal or non metal
Nitrogen	14	7	7	7	7	Non-metal

5. From the orbital picture of an element answer the following questions.

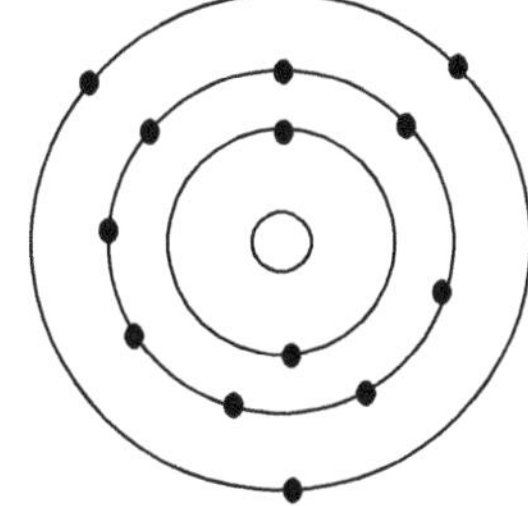

(i) How many electrons present in M shell?

(ii) Name the element.

(iii) Name the element that undergoes oxidation or reduction. Give reason.

(iv) What is the number of protons of the element?

Ans. (i) M shell is the third shell. So, number of electrons in M shell is three.

(ii) The element is aluminium.

(iii) Aluminium atom can donate three electrons from the valence shell. So, it undergoes oxidation.

(iv) The number of protons is equal to number of electrons.

6. Complete the following table.

Number of protons	Number of electrons	Name of the element
12	(i)	(ii)
(iii)	20	(iv)

Ans.

Number of protons	Number of electrons	Name of the element
12	12	Magnesium
20	20	Calcium

7. Complete the table given below:

Isotope	Symbolic representation	Protons	Electrons	Neutron
Protium	${}^{1}_{1}H$			
Deuterium	${}^{2}_{1}H$			
Tritium	${}^{3}_{1}H$			

Ans.

Isotope	Symbolic representation	Protons	Electrons	Neutron
Protium	${}^{1}_{1}H$	1	1	0
Deuterium	${}^{2}_{1}H$	1	1	1
Tritium	${}^{3}_{1}H$	1	1	2

Chapter 5. The Periodic Table

1. The positions of elements are shown in the table.

Group 1	Group 2	Group 17	Group 18
	B		
A			D
		C	

Observe the above table and answer the following questions.

(i) Which element is/are non-metal?

(ii) How many valence electrons A has?

(iii) What is the valency of D?

(iv) How many electrons does C need to complete octet?

Ans.

1. (i) C and D (ii) One (iii) Zero (iv) 1
2. Complete the following table.

Element	Electronic	Type of element
Neon		
Magnesium		

Ans.

Element	Electronic configuration	Type of element
Neon	2, 8	Inert gas
Magnesium	2, 8, 2	Alkali metal

3.

Atomic number	Element	Electronic configuration	Select element of the same group
11	Sodium		(Ca/N/K).........
15	Phosphorus		(Al/N/C)..........
16	Sulphur		(F/Cl/O)............
9	Fluorine		(Ca/Cl/K)........

Ans.

Atomic number	Element	Electronic configuration	Select element of the same group
11	Sodium	2, 8, 1	K
15	Phosphorus	2, 8, 5	N
16	Sulphur	2, 8, 6	O
9	Fluroine	2, 7	Cl

4. Complete the table: [Annual Exam 2019]

Element	Mass No.	Atomic No.	No. of electrons	No. of neutrons	Electronic configuration
Potassium	39	19			

Ans.

Element	Mass No.	Atomic No.	No. of electrons	No. of neutrons	Electronic configuration
Potassium	39	19	19	20	2,8,8,1

5. A part of the periodic table has been shown below:

Group / Period	1	2			13	14	15	16	17	18
1										
2	A	C							E	G
3	B					D			F	

Answer the following questions on the basis of position of elements in the given table.

(i) Which element in the given table.

(ii) Which element is most electronegative? Give reason.

(iii) Write the electronic configuration of (a) B and (b) E.

Ans. (i) G is a noble gas because it is present in group 18 and has zero valency.

(ii) E is the most electronegative element due to its smallest atomic size and more electron affinity.

(iii) (a) Electronic configuration of B: K L M
2, 8, 1

(b) Electronic configuration of E: K L
2, 7

6. The position of three elements A, B and C in the periodic table are shown below.

Group 16	Group 17
	A
B	C

(i) State whether A is a metal or non-metal.

(ii) State whether C is more reactive or less reactive than A.

(iii) Will C be larger or smaller in size than B?

(iv) Which type of ion, cation or anion, will be formed by A?

Ans. (i) Since, A belongs to group 17 and has 7 valence electrons so, it is a non-metal because it will gain electrons to complete its octet.

(ii) C lies below A and in the same group. As we move down in a group, the size increases and electronegative character decreases. With the increase in electronegative character, the electron adapting tendency and hence the reactivity decrease, so C is less reactive than A.

(iii) C is smaller than B in size because as we move left to right in a period atomic size decreases due to increased effective nuclear charge.

(iv) As discussed in part (i) that element A has a tendency to gain electron to complete its octet. It needs to take up one electron., so it will form anion (A^-).

Chapter 6. Hydrogen

1. Complete the following table.

Impurities present with hydrogen	Solution used to remove it
Hydrogen sulphide	
Carbon dioxide	
Sulphur dioxide	
Phosphine	

Ans.

Impurities present with hydrogen	Solution used to remove it
Hydrogen sulphide	Lead nitrate
Carbon dioxide	Caustic potash
Sulphur dioxide	Caustic potash
Phosphine	Silver nitrate

2. Complete the following table.

Element	Oxidising/Reducing agent
Manganese dioxide	
Chlorine	

Hydrogen sulphide	
Hydrogen peroxide	

Ans.

Element	Oxidising/Reducing agent
Manganese dioxide	Oxidising agent
Chlorine	Oxidising agent
Hydrogen sulphide	Reducing agent
Hydrogen peroxide	Oxidising agent

Chapter 7. Study of Gas Laws

1. Complete the following table.

Gas laws	Mathematical representation	Constant variables
Boyle's law		
Charles law		

Ans.

Gas laws	Mathematical representation	Constant variables
Boyle's law	$P_1V_1 = P_2V_2$	Temperature
Charles law	$\frac{V_1}{T_1} = \frac{V_2}{T_2}$	Pressure

2. Observe the following graph carefully and answer the following questions.

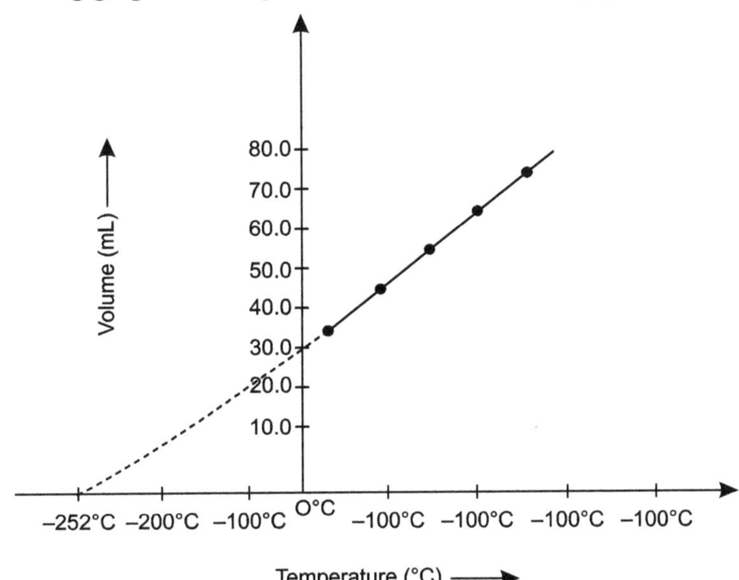

(i) Name the gas law for which the graph is made.
(ii) What is the general term used for this type of graphs?
(iii) How the volume of gas is related to the temperature according to the graph?
(iv) Give the mathematical representation of the gas law for which the graph is made.

Ans. (i) Charles' law (ii) Isobar

(iii) According to the graph, the volume of the gas increases on increasing temperature.

(iv) The graph represents Charles' law. So, mathematical representation is $\frac{V_1}{T_1} = \frac{V_2}{T_2}$.

Chapter 8. Atmospheric Pollution

1. Complete the following table.

Pollutant	Origin	Impact
Suspended particulate matter		Damage functioning of lungs.
	Present in petrol, diesel, paint and batteries.	Damages the nervous and digestive system.
Carbon monoxide	Incomplete burning of petrol, diesel, wood and tobacco.	
	Released by refrigerators and air conditioning systems.	Reduces ozone layer.

Ans.

Pollutant	Origin	Impact
Suspended particulate matter	Solids suspended in smoke, dust and vapour.	Damage functioning of lungs.
Lead	Present in petrol, diesel, paint and batteries.	Damages the nervous and digestive system.
Carbon monoxide	Incomplete burning of petrol, diesel, wood and tobacco.	Reduces oxygen in blood causing retardation and dizziness.
Chlorofluorocarbon (CFC)	Released by refrigerators and air conditioning systems.	Reduces ozone layer.

❑

Short Answer Type Questions

| Set 14 |

Chapter 1. The Language of Chemistry

1. Define variable valency.

Ans. Some elements exhibit more than on valency. This phenomenon is called variable valency. For example; iron, copper etc.

2. What is the name fundamental law that is involved in writing a chemical reaction?

Ans. Law of conservation of matter.

3. When an element is said that it shows variable valency?

Ans. An atom of an element can sometimes lose more electrons that are present in its valence shell *i.e.*, there is a loss of electrons from the penultimate shell too. Then, the elements is said that it shows variable valency.

4. Why an equation should be balanced?

Ans. An equation must be balanced in order to comply with the 'law of conservation of matter', which states that matter is neither created nor destroyed in the course of a chemical reaction. An unbalanced equation would imply that atoms have been created or destroyed.

5. What do you mean by 'amu'?

Ans. Atomic mass unit (amu) is equal to one twelfth the mass of an atom of carbon-12.

6. The chemical symbol for sodium is Na and for silicon it is Si but for sulphur symbol is S. Explain.

Ans. Generally each element is denoted by a symbol, which is usually the first letter of its name in English or Latin, written in capital. The chemical symbol for sodium is Na (taken from its Latin name natrium), for sulphur is S (taken the first letter of the English name sulphur) and for silicon symbol is Si as there is already an element present whose first letter is also S (Sulphur). So, first two letter of the silicon is used to give the symbol for silicon. Second letter is written in small.

7. Discuss the naming of elements with variable valency. Give example.

Ans. When some elements exhibit more than one valency they show variable valency. If the element exhibit two different positive valencies, then suffix 'ous' is used for the lower valency and the suffix 'ic' is used for higher valency. Modern chemist use roman numerals in place of the trivial name. For example, in the compound Fe_2O_3, in which the element shows variable valency (2, 3). In this compound, valency of iron is +3 (higher one). So, suffix 'ic' is used. Hence, name of the compound is ferric oxide. The name used by modern chemists is [Iron (III)] oxide.

8. Write the valency of the following:

(i) Fluorine in CaF_2

(ii) Carbon in CH_4

(iii) Phosphorus in PH_3

Ans.

Name of the compound	Exchange valencies	Valency
(i) CaF_2	$Ca^2\ F^1$	Valency of calcium is +2
(ii) CH_4	$C^4\ H^1$	Valency of carbon is 4
(iii) PH_3	$P^3\ H^1$	Valency of phosphorus is 3

9. An element 'X' forms an oxide XO.

(i) What is the valency of X?

(ii) What will be the formula of fluoride of X.

Ans. (i) Valency of X is 2.

(ii) The formula fluoride of X is XF_2.

10. Arrange the following elements in increasing order of their valencies.

Magnesium, aluminium, oxygen, helium.

Ans. Helium < Magnesium < Oxygen < Aluminium

11. An element 'Z' forms the following compounds with hydrogen, carbon and oxygen as H_2Z, CZ_2, ZO_2, ZO_3. State the three valencies of the element Z which are illustrated by these compound.

Ans.

Compound	Exchange valencies	Valency of Z
H_2Z	$H^1\ Z^1$	1
CZ_2	$C^2\ Z^1$	1
ZO_2	$Z^2\ O^1$	2
ZO_3	$Z^3\ O^1$	3

Hence, the three valencies of Z is 1, 2 and 3.

12. Write about the disadvantages of hit and trial method of balancing the equations.

Ans. Disadvantages of hit and trial method of balancing equations are:

(i) It takes time to balance complicated equations.

(ii) The mechanism (Steps of the reaction, *i.e.,* how the reaction takes place) of the reaction is not clear.

13. What would be wrong, if we write CO for cobalt instead of Co?

Ans. In chemical symbol of elements, first letter is always in capital letter and second letter is in small letter. So , if we write CO for the element cobalt, it is wrong. So symbol for cobalt is Co.

14. A compound is formed by two element A and B. The valency of A and B is 3 and 2 respectively. What is the molecular formula of the compound?

Ans.

Compound with valencies	Exchange of valencies	Molecular formula
A^3B^2	A^2B^3	A_2B_3

So, molecular formula of the compound is A_2B_3.

15. Correct the following statements.

(i) An element is represented by molecular formula.

(ii) H_2O_2 is the molecular formula of water.

(iii) Sulphur is a monoatomic molecule.

(iv) Chemical symbol for cobalt is CO.

(v) Formula of ferric oxide is FeO.

Ans. (i) A molecule is represented by molecular formula.

(ii) H_2O is the molecular formula of water.

(iii) Sulphur is octatomic molecule.

(iv) Chemical symbol for cobalt is Co.

(v) Formula of ferric oxide is Fe_2O_3.

16. Write the empirical formula of the following:

(i) Benzene (C_6H_6) (ii) Glucose ($C_6H_{12}O_6$) (iii) Acetylene (C_2H_2)

(iv) Acetic acid (CH_3COOH)

Ans. The empirical formula of a compound is the simplest formula which gives the simplest ratio in whole numbers of atoms different elements present in one molecule of the compound.

(i) The empirical formula of Benzene (C_6H_6) is CH. It indicates the simplest ratio of 1: 1.

(ii) The empirical formula of Glucose ($C_6H_{12}O_6$) is CH_2O. It indicates the simplest ratio of 1: 2: 1.

(iii) The empirical formula of Acetylene (C_2H_2) is CH. It indicates the simples ratio of 1: 1.

(iv) The empirical formula of Acetic acid (CH_3COOH or C_2H_4O) is CH_2O. It indicates the simplest ratio of 1: 2: 1.

17. What are polyatomic ions? Give example.

Ans. Polyatomic ion is a charged chemical species composed of two or more atoms. For example; bicarbonate ion (HCO_3^-), acetate ion (CH_3COO^-), etc.

18. Give some significance of molecular formula.

Ans. Significance of molecular formula are:

(i) It represents both the molecule and the molecular mass of the compound.

(ii) It represents the respective numbers of different atoms present in one molecule of the compound.

(iii) It represents the ratio of the respective masses of the elements present in the compound.

19. What is the valency of nitrogen in the following compounds?

(i) N_2O_3 (ii) N_2O_5 (iii) NO (iv) NO_2

Compound	Exchange valencies	Valency of N
NO_2	$N^{2\times2}$ $O^{1\times2}$	4

Ans. (i)

Compound	Exchange valencies	Valency of N
N_2O_3	N^3 O^2	3

(ii)

Compount	Exchange valencies	Valency of N
N_2O_5	N^5 O^2	5

(iii)

Compound	Exchange valencies	Valency of N
NO	$N^{2\times1}$ $O^{2\times1}$	2

20. Give one example of each of the following:

(i) An acidic radical that is trivalent.

(ii) A basic radical that is divalent.

(iii) An acidic radical of valency one. **[November, 2019]**

Ans. (i) Phosphite (PO_3^{3-})

(ii) Calcium (Ca^{+2})

(iii) Chlorine (Cl^-)

Chapter 2. Chemical Change and Reaction

1. Write about the conditions necessary for a chemical change.

Ans. The necessary conditions for a chemical change are:

(i) Mixing, (ii) Solution, (iii) Heat, (iv) Light, (v) Electricity, (vi) Pressure.

2. How photochemical reaction takes place?

Ans. In the photochemical reaction, molecules of reactants absorb light energy to get activated and then react rapidly.

3. What are the characteristics of chemical reaction?

Ans. Characteristics of chemical reaction are:

(i) Evolution of gas, (ii) Change of colour, (iii) Formation of precipitate, (iv) Change of state

4. Burning of hydrogen in oxygen gives water and passing of electricity through water gives hydrogen and oxygen. Name the type of chemical change involved in the two cases.

Ans. Burning of hydrogen in oxygen gives water, so it is a combination reaction and passing of electricity through water gives hydrogen and oxygen, so it is a decomposition reaction.

5. How thermal dissociation is different from thermal decomposition?

Ans. A simultaneous reversible decomposition reaction brought about only by heat is called thermal dissociation.

A decomposition reaction that is brought about by heat without any recombination on cooling is called thermal decomposition.

6. What are the uses of neutralisation reaction in day-to-day life?

Ans. Some uses of neutralisation reaction in daily life are:

(i) When someone is stung by bee, formic acid enters the skin and gives pain, which can be relieved by rubbing the spot with slaked lime or baking soda, both of which are basic in nature.

(ii) If the soil is somewhat acidic and thus unfavourable for growing certain crops, slaked lime is added to neutralise the excess acid.

7. Give an example of a reaction where the following conditions are involved.

(i) Heat, (ii) Light, (iii) Electricity, (iv) Close contact, (v) Pressure, (vi) Catalyst.

Ans. (i) Heat

$$CuCO_3(s) \xrightarrow{\Delta} CuO(s) + CO_2(g)$$

(ii) Light

$$6CO_2 + 12H_2O \xrightarrow{\text{Light}} C_6H_{12}O_6 + CO_2 + 6H_2O$$

(iii) Electricity

$$2NaCl \xrightarrow{\text{Electricity}} 2Na + Cl_2$$

(iv) Close contact

$$NaCl(aq) + AgNO_3(aq) \longrightarrow \underbrace{AgCl}_{\text{White ppt.}} + NaNO_3(aq)$$

(v) Pressure

$$N_2 + 3H_2 \xrightleftharpoons{\text{Above 200 atm}} 2NH_3$$

(vi) Catalyst

$$Pb(NO_3)_2(s) + 2KI(s) \rightarrow 2KNO_3(s) + PbI_2(s)$$

8. Write the chemical reaction where the following changes are observed.

(i) Gas is evolved , (ii) Colour change is observed, (iii) Precipitate is formed.

Ans. (i) When zinc carbonate is heated, carbon dioxide gas is evolved.

$$ZnCO_3 \rightarrow ZnO + CO_2\uparrow$$

(ii) When hydrated copper sulphate is heated, colour change is observed.

$$\underbrace{u \quad _4 \quad _2()}_{\text{Blue}} \rightarrow \underbrace{u \quad _4(s)}_{\text{White}} \quad _2(g)$$

(iii) When barium chloride reacts with sodium sulphate, precipitate is formed.

$$BaCl_2\,(aq) + Na_2SO_4(aq) \rightarrow \underbrace{BaSO_4(s)}_{\text{White ppt.}} + 2NaCl$$

9. Give an example of an endothermic and exothermic reaction involving carbon as one of the reactants.

Ans. An endothermic reaction is the reaction in which heat is abosrbed.

$$2C(s) + O_2(g) \rightarrow 2CO$$

An exothermic reaction is the reaction in which heat is liberated.

$$C(s) + O_2(g) \rightarrow CO_2$$

10. What do you mean by reversible reaction?

Ans. The type of reaction in which the direction of chemical change can be reversed by changing the conditions under which the reaction is taking place is called reversible reaction.

11. Why energy is involved in a chemical change?

Ans. A chemical reaction involves the breaking up of chemical bonds between atoms resulting in absorption of energy in the form of heat and simultaneously formation of bonds with release of energy. These two types of energy are different from each other, *i.e.*, there is either a surplus or a deficit of energy during the reaction. Therefore, in a chemical reaction energy is either absorbed or released.

12. Give an example of an exothermic reaction of nature.

Ans. Respiration.

13. Give one example of a reaction where the following cases involved.

(i) Evolution of heat , (ii) Absorption of heat, and (iii) High pressure is required.

Ans. (i) Evolution of heat:

$$\underbrace{CaO}_{\text{Quicklime}} + H_2O \longrightarrow \underbrace{Ca\,(OH)_2}_{\text{Slaked lime}} + \text{Heat}$$

(ii) Absorption of heat:

$$C + 2S \xrightarrow{\Delta} CS_2$$

(iii) High pressure is required:

$$N_2 + 3H_2 \underset{}{\overset{\text{above 200 atm}}{\rightleftharpoons}} 2NH_3$$

14. Identify the type of reaction for the following:

(i) $Cl_2 + 2KBr \rightarrow 2KCl + Br_2$

(ii) $2HgO \rightarrow 2Hg + O_2$

(iii) $Fe + CuSO_4 \rightarrow FeSO_4 + Cu$

(iv) $AgNO_3 + NaCl \rightarrow AgCl + NaNO_3$

(v) $PbO_2 + SO_2 \rightarrow PbSO_4$

Ans. (i) Displacement reaction

(ii) Decomposition reaction

(iii) Displacement reaction

(iv) Double displacement reaction

(v) Combination reaction

15. What is precipitation reaction? Give an example.

Ans. A chemical reaction in which two compounds in their aqueous state react to form an insoluble salt (a precipitate) as one of the product is known as precipitation reaction.

$$CuSO_4(aq) + H_2S(g) \rightarrow \underbrace{CuS(s)}_{\text{Black ppt.}} + H_2SO_4(aq)$$

16. Arrange the elements (K, H, Na, Cu) in increasing order of reactivity.

Ans. Order of reactivities are followed as: Cu < H < Na < K.

17. What is synthesis?

Ans. Synthesis is a reaction in which two or more substance combine together to form a single substance.

18. How decomposition reaction takes place?

Ans. Decomposition reaction takes place in the presence of heat or light, or by the passage of an electric current.

19. Photosynthesis is an example of combination reaction. Explain.

Ans. Photosynthesis is an example of combination reaction because in this reaction carbon dioxide reacts with water to produce glucose.

20. Give an example of a reaction involving:

(i) Blue solution, (ii) Formation of a dirty green precipitate.

Ans. (i) Blue solution

$$Fe + \underbrace{CuSO_4(aq)}_{\text{Blue solution}} \longrightarrow \underbrace{FeSO_4}_{\text{Green solution}} + Cu$$

(ii) Dirty green precipitate is formed.

$$FeSO_4 + 2\,NaO \longrightarrow Fe(OH)_2 + Na_2SO_4$$

21. Give an example of photochemical reaction involving:

(i) Silver salt, (ii) Water

Ans. (i) Silver salt

$$2AgNO_3 \xrightarrow{\text{Sunlight}} 2Ag + 2NO_2 + O_3$$

(ii) Water

$$6CO_2 + 12H_2O \xrightarrow{\text{Light}} C_6H_{12}O_6 + CO_2 + 6H_2O$$

22. State the colour of:

(i) The residue when copper carbonate is heated.

(ii) The flame when flame test is perfomed with potassium nitrate.

(iii) The solution when few pieces of iron is dropped into copper sulphate solution.

(iv) The potassium permanganate solution when sulphur dioxide gas passes through it.

(v) The flame when flame test is performed with potassium nitrate. **[November, 2019]**

(vi) The residue when lead nitrate is decomposed on heating. **[November, 2019]**

Ans. (i) Black (ii) Violet

(iii) Light green (iv) Colourless

(v) Colour of the flame obtained is purple when flame test is performed on potassium nitrate.

(vi) Colour of the residue obtained is yellow when the lead nitrate is decomposed on heating.

$$\underset{\text{(Lead nitrate)}}{2Pb(NO_3)(s)} \xrightarrow{\text{Heat}} \underset{\text{(Lead oxide)}}{2PbO(s)} + \underset{\text{(Nitrogen dioxide)}}{4NO_2(g)} + \underset{\text{(Oxygen)}}{O_2(g)}$$

23. Referring to carbon dioxide gas, answer the following questions.

(i) Its colour. (ii) Its reaction with litmus paper.

(iii) Its reaction when passes through lime water (iv) Write the reaction for part (iii).

Ans. (i) It is colourless. (ii) It turns moist blue litmus faint red.

(iii) When carbon dioxide gas passes through lime water, it turns milky due to the formation of white precipitate.

(iv) $Ca(OH)_2 + CO_2 \rightarrow CaCO_3 \downarrow + H_2O$

24. Classify the following as Combination; Displacement; Decomposition and Double Decomposition reactions: **[November, 2019]**

(i) $Zn + 2HCl \rightarrow ZnCl_2 + H_2$ (ii) $4Na + O_2 \rightarrow 2Na_2O$

(iii) $NaCl + AgNO_3 \rightarrow AgCl + NaNO_3$ (iv) $4HNO_3 \rightarrow 4NO_2 + 2H_2O + O_2$

Ans. (i) $Zn + 2HCl \rightarrow ZnCl_2 + H_2$ is a Displacement reaction.

(ii) $4\,Na + O_2 \rightarrow 2Na_2O$ is a Combination reaction.

(iii) $NaCl + AgNO_3 \rightarrow AgCl + NaNO_3$ is a Double displacement reaction.

(iv) $4\,HNO_3 \rightarrow 4NO_2 + 2H_2O + O_2$ is a Decomposition reaction.

25. Classify the following reactions as Direct combination Decomposition, Displacement, Precipitation and Neutralisation. **[February, 2020]**

(i) $Fe + CuSO_4 \rightarrow FeSO_4 + Cu$

(ii) $2Pb\,(NO_3)_2 \rightarrow 2PbO + 4NO_2 \uparrow + O_2 \uparrow$

(iii) $2Mg + O_2 \rightarrow 2\,MgO$

(iv) $Na_2SO_4 + Pb(NO_3)_2 \rightarrow PbSO_4 + 2\,NaNO_3$

Ans. (i) $Fe + CuSO_4 \rightarrow FeSO_4 + Cu$; This is a displacement reaction.

(ii) $2Pb(NO_3)_2 \rightarrow 2\,PbO + 4\,NO_2 + O_2 \uparrow$; This is a decomposition reaction.

(iii) $2\,Mg + O_2 \rightarrow MgO$; This is a direct combination reaction.

(iv) $Na_2SO_4 + Pb(NO_3)_2 \rightarrow PbSO_4 + 2NaNO_3$; This is a displacement reaction.

26. (i) Why do we store silver chloride in dark coloured bottles?

(ii) Why is photosynthesis considered an endothermic reaction?

Ans. (i) Dark coloured bottles interrupt the parth of light such that light cannot reach to silver chloride contained in the bottles and its decomposition is prevented. It is known that silver chloride decomposes to silver and chlorine in the presence of light.

(ii) Photosynthesis is considered as an endothermic reaction because energy in the form of sunlight is absorbed by the green plants.

27. Arrange the following metals in the decreasing order of reactivity Na, K, Cu and Ag.

Ans. The decreasing order of reactivity of the given metals is K > Na > Cu > Ag.

28. Identify the type of reaction in the following examples.

(i) $Na_2SO_4(aq) + BaCl_2(aq) \longrightarrow BaSO_4(s) + 2NaCl\,(aq)$

(ii) $Fe(s) + CuSO_4(aq) \longrightarrow FeSO_4(aq) + Cu(s)$

(iii) $2H_2(g) + O_2(g) \longrightarrow 2H_2O(l)$

Ans. (i) Double displacement reaction.

(ii) Displacement reaction.

(iii) Combination reaction.

29. Why does the colour of copper sulphate solution change when an iron nail is dipped in it?

Ans. The colour of copper sulphate solution changes when an iron nail is dipped in it because iron being more reactive than copper, displaces copper metal from aqueous copper sulphate solution. Thus, blue colour of copper sulphate disappears and green colour of ferrous sulphate is formed.

$$\underset{\text{Iron}}{Fe(s)} + \underset{\text{Blue}}{CuSO_4(aq)} \longrightarrow \underset{\text{Ferrous sulphate}}{FeSO_4(aq)} + \underset{\text{Copper}}{Cu}$$

30. What happens when dilute hydrochloric acid is added to iron fillings?

Ans. Iron being a reactive metal which produces H_2 gas along with its salt, where iron (II) chloride is formed on reaction with dilute hydrochloric acid. This is a displacement reaction.

$$\underset{\text{Iron}}{Fe(s)} + 2HCl\,(aq) \longrightarrow \underset{\text{Iron (II) chloride}}{FeCl_2(aq)} + \underset{\text{Hydrogen}}{H_2(g)}$$

31. When solutions of silver nitrate and potassium chloride are mixed, a white precipitate forms. The ionic equation for the reaction is $Ag^+(aq) + Cl^- \longrightarrow AgCl(s)$

(i) (a) What is the name of the white precipitate?

(b) It its a soluble or insoluble compounds?

(ii) Is the precipitation of silver chloride a redox reactions?

Ans. (i) (a) White precipitate of silver chloride (AgCl) is formed.

(b) Silver chloride (AgCl) is an insoluble compound.

(ii) It is not a redox reaction. In this reaction, cations Ag^+ and N^{3+} have exchanged their anions NO^{-3} and Cl^- and a precipitate of AgCl has been formed.

$$\underset{\text{Sodium chloride}}{NaCl_{(aq)}} + \underset{\text{Silver nitrate}}{AgNO_3(aq)} \longrightarrow \underset{\text{Silver chloride}}{AgCl(s)} + \underset{\text{Sodium nitrate}}{NaNO_3(aq)}$$

Chapter 3. Water

1. Name the gas evolved when potassium nitrate is heated.

Ans. Oxygen.

2. How can the gases can be dried?

Ans. Gases can be dried by passing the gases through conc. sulphuric acid as it has strong affinity for water, so it easily extracts water from many substances.

3. How does hard water check lead poisoning?

Ans. Hard water checks the poisoning of water by lead pipes. When these pipes are used for carrying water, some lead salts dissolve in water to make it poisonous. Calcium sulphate present in hard water forms insoluble lead sulphate in the form of layer inside the lead pipe and this checks lead poisoning.

4. Why does washing soda coat with a white powder when left exposed to the atmosphere?

Ans. Washing soda is efflorescent substance. So, it loses water of crystallisation partly when exposed to atomosphere and change into white powder.

5. 'Water is considered as a universal solvent'. Explain.

Ans. Water dissolves many substances forming aqueous solutions. In water, not only solids but gases and other liquids are also dissolved. Therefore, water is called a universal solvent.

6. Explain the effect of temperature on solubility of KNO_3 and $CaSO_4$ in water.

Ans. Solubility of KNO_3 in water increases with increase in temperature and solubility of $CaSO_4$ in water decreases with increase in temperature.

7. What is water of crystallisation?

Ans. The fixed amount of water that is associated with some compounds which are integral part of their crystalline structure is called water of cystallisation.

8. Mention three factors which affect the solubility of solid solute in a solvent.

Ans. Factors which affect the solubility of a solid solute in a solvent are:

(i) Size of particle, (ii) Temperature, and (iii) Stirring

9. Write the chemical formula of the following:

(i) Glauber's salt (ii) Potash alum

Ans. (i) Glauber's salt: $Na_2SO_4.10H_2O$

(ii) Potash alum: $K_2SO_4.Al_2(SO_4)_3.24H_2O$

10. On cooling, hot saturated solution of potassium nitrate forms crystal. Explain.

Ans. With a decrease in temperature, the solubility of potassium nitrate decreases. Hence, when a saturated solution of potassium nitrate cools excess of nitrate separates from the solution to form crystals.

11. Addition of washing soda removes hardness of water. Explain.

Ans. When washing soda or soda ash is added to hard water, the corresponding insoluble carbonates settle down and can be removed by filtration.

$$Ca(HCO_3)_2 + Na_2CO_3 \rightarrow CaCO_3 \downarrow + 2NaHCO_3$$
$$Mg(HCO_3)_2 + Na_2CO_3 \rightarrow MgCO_3 \downarrow + 2NaHCO_3$$

12. Write three characteristics of a solution.

Ans. Following are the characteristics of a solution:

(i) The solute particles in a solution do not settle down.

(ii) Its components cannot be separated by filtration.

(iii) It does not scatter light.

13. Define latent heat of vapourisation of water. What is the specific value of latent heat of vapourisation of water?

Ans. Latent heat of vaporisation of water is the energy required to change water into its vapour at its boiling point without any change in temperature. The specific value of latent heat of vaporisation of water is 2268 J/g.

14. (i) Name the process of removal of hardness by adding lime?

(ii) Why do permanent hardness of water take place?

Ans. (i) Clark's process.

(ii) Permanent hardness is due to the presence of chlorides and sulphates of calcium and magnesium.

15. Why does table salt get sticky on exposure to humid air during the stormy season? Explain.

Ans. Table salt contains small amount impurities like magnesium chloride and calcium chloride, which are deliquescent substance. This will make the table salt absorb moisture in rainy season to turn it sticky.

16. (i) How can we know a solution is saturated solution?

(ii) How can a saturated solution be converted into unsaturated solution?

Ans. (i) A solution is called saturated solution if more solute is not possible to be dissolved in the solution.

(ii) A saturated solution is converted into unsaturated solution by the following two ways:

(a) By adding solvent, (b) By heating the solution, or (c) By increasing temperature.

17. Write the product of the following reactions:

(i) $Na_2SO_4.10H_2O \xrightarrow{\text{Dry air}}$ (ii) N $\xrightarrow{\text{Heat}}$

(iii) $CuSO_4.5H_2O \xrightarrow{\text{Conc. } H_2SO}$

Ans. (i) $Na_2SO_4.10H_2O \xrightarrow{\text{Dry air}} Na_2SO_4 + 10H_2O$

(ii) $\underbrace{2KNO_3}_{\text{Potassium nitrate}} \xrightarrow{\text{Heat}} \underbrace{2KNO_2}_{\text{Potassium nitrite}} + O_2\uparrow$

(iii) $CuSO_4.5H_2O \xrightarrow{2\ \ 4} \underbrace{\quad 4}_{\text{white}} \quad 2$

18. What is permutit method. How can it be used for softening hard water?

Ans. Permutit is an artificial zeolite. Chemically, it is hydrated sodium aluminium orthosilicate with the formula $Na_2Al_2Si_2O_8\,xH_2O$. For Example:

A tall cylinder is loosely filled with lomps of permutit. Ions get exchanged when hard water containing calcium and magnesium permutit and water becomes soft on removal of calcium and magnesium ions. When no longer active, permutit regenerates by running a concentrated solution of brine on it and removing calcium chloride formed by repeatition of washing.

$$CaP + 2\,NaCl \rightarrow Na_2P + CaCl_2$$

19. How is calcium and magnesium ion present in hard water helpful for us?

Ans. Calcium and magnesium salts present in small amounts in hard water are essential for the growth of our bones and teeth.

20. Write any two advantages of hard water.

Ans. Advantages of hard water are:

(i) Presence of salts and ions in hard water makes it tasty.

(ii) Hard water checks poisoning of water by lead pipes.

21. Why do rivers and lakes not freeze easily?

Ans. Rivers and lakes do not freeze easily because of high specific latent heat of solidification of water.

22. Explain the terms:

(i) Solution (ii) Solute (iii) Solvent

Ans. (i) A solution is a homogeneous mixture consists of two or more components whose composition may be changed by changing the relative amounts of the components.

(ii) The small amount of substance which dissolves in a solvent is called solute.

(iii) A solvent is the medium where one or more components are dissolved to form a solution.

23. Solubility of NaCl at 40°C is 36.5 g. What is meant by this statements?

Ans. Solubility of NaCl at 40°C is 36.5 g means 36.5 g of NaCl dissolves in 100 g of water at a temperature of 40°C.

24. What are stalagmites and stalacitites and how are they formed?

Ans. In some limestone caves conical pillar-like objects hanging from the roof of the caves and some are rising from the floor. These are formed by water containing dissolved calcium hydrogen carbonate which are continuously dropping from the cracks in the rocks. Release of pressure results in the conversion of some hydrogen carbonate to calcium carbonate.

$$Ca(HCO_3)_2 \rightarrow CaCO_3 + CO_2 + H_2O$$

This calcium carbonate little by little and slowly deposit on both roof and floor of the cave. The conical pillar which grows downwards from the roof is called stalactite and the one which grows upward from the floor of the cave is called stalagmite.

25. Give equations to show what happens when temporary hard water is:

(i) Boiled (ii) Treated with slaked lime

Ans. (i) $Ca(HCO_3)_2 \xrightarrow{\text{Boil}} CaCO_3 \downarrow + H_2O + CO_2 \uparrow$

$Mg(HCO_3)_2 \xrightarrow{\text{Boil}} MgCO_3 \downarrow + H_2O + CO_2 \uparrow$

(ii) $Ca(HCO_3)_2 + Ca(OH)_2 \longrightarrow 2CaCO_3 \downarrow + 2H_2O$

$Mg(HCO_3)_2 + Ca(OH)_2 \longrightarrow MgCO_3 \downarrow + CaCO_3 \uparrow + 2H_2O$

26. State the colour of the residue when hydrated copper sulphate crystals are heated. [Novmber 2019]

Ans. The colour of the residue obtained is white when the hydrated copper sulphate crystals are heated:

$$\underset{\text{Blue crystals}}{CuSO_4.5H_2O} \xrightarrow{\text{Heat}} \underset{\text{White crystals}}{CuSO_4 + 5H_2O}$$

27. Give one example of each of the following: **[November, 2019]**

(i) An efflorescent substance. (ii) A liquid dehydrating agent

(iii) A solid hygroscopic substance (iv) A non-metallic reducing agent

Ans. (i) Efflorescent substance – $Na_2SO_4.10H_2O$ (Sodium sulphate)

(ii) Liquid dehydrating agent – H_2SO_4 (Sulphuric acid)

(iii) A solid hygroscopic substance – Anhydrous calcium carbonate ($CaCO_3$)

(iv) A non-metallic reducing agent – H_2 (Dihydrogen)

28. (i) What is hard water? **[November, 2019]**

(ii) Write a balanced equation for removal of temporary hardness.

(iii) Write one disadvantage of hard water.

Ans. (i) Hard water contains a high amount of dissolved minierals, mainly calcium and magnesium ions (in the form of bicarbonates) and some other traces of metals. Hard water is unfit for drinking and washing purposes.

(ii) Temporary hardness can be removed by boiling the water sample.

$$Ca(HCO_3)_2 \xrightarrow{\text{Heat}} CaCO_3 + H_2O + CO_2$$

(iii) One disadvantage of hard water is that it causes incrustation in water carrying pipes and pipes get clogged due to precipitation of salts. **[February, 2020]**

29. (i) What causes permanent hardness in water?

(ii) State one advantage of using hard water.

(iii) Give an equation for the removal of permanent hardness in water.

Ans. (i) Permanent hardness of water is caused by dissolved chlorides, sulphates and nitrates of calcium and magnesium. This is not removed by boiling.

(ii) One advantage of hard water is that it does not dissolve lead (Pb) in water and as a result of this it does not lead to lead poisoning.

(iii) One method to remove permanent hardness of water is treatment with sodium carbonate which converts calcium and magnesium salts to insoluble carbonates which can be filtered off.

$$CaCl_2(aq) + Na_2CO_3 \longrightarrow CaCO_3\ (s) \downarrow + NaCl\ (aq)$$

Chapter 4. Atomic Structure and Chemical Bonding

1. Mass of an atom is concentrated in the nucleus. Explain.

Ans. Mass number of an element is the total number of protons and neutrons in the nucleus. Hence, mass of an atom is concentrated in the nucleus.

2. State the type of bond in sodium chloride.

Ans. Sodium chloride is an ionic compound. So, type of bond in sodium chloride is ionic or electrovalent bond.

3. Sulphur has atomic number of 16 and mass number of 32. State the number of protons and neutrons in the nucleus of sulphur. Give a simple diagram to show the arrangement of electrons in an atom of sulphur.

Ans. Atomic number of sulphur is 16. So, number of protons in sulphur are 16.

Number of neutrons = Mass number – Atomic number

= 32 – 16 = 16

4. An element A has one electron in its first shell. It combines with element B having 7 electrons in its third shell. What type of bond is formed?

Ans. The type of bond formed is covalent bond.

5. What type of bonds present in:

(i) ethene, and (ii) ethyne?

Ans. (i) Double bond and (ii) Triple bond.

6. Name two compounds that are covalent when taken pure but produce ions when dissolved in water.

Ans. Ammonia and HCl.

7. How hydrogen combines with all non-metals?

Ans. Hydrogen can combine with all non-metals with the help of covalent bonds.

8. The atomic number and mass number of sodium are 11 and 23 respectively. What information is conveyed by this statement?

Ans. The atomic number of sodium is 11, that means number of electrons and protons in sodium are 11 and mass number is 13 that means number of nucleons (protons and neutrons) in sodium are 23. So, the number is 23, number of neutrons are 12 (Number of neutrons = Number of protons + Number of neutrons).

9. An atom X has three electrons more than the noble gas configuration. What type of ion will it form?

Ans. X can form lose three electrons. So, it can form cation.

10. What type of compounds are usually formed between metals and non-metals and why?

Ans. The bonds formed between metals and non-metals are ionic or electrovalent bonds.

The metals have one, two or three electrons in their valence shell. They have tendency to lose their valence electrons. So, they combine with non-metals which have five, six or seven electrons in their valence shell and thus have tendency to gain electrons and form ionic bonds.

11. The electronic configuration of fluoride ion is the same as that of a neon atom. What is the difference between these two atoms?

Ans. Neon is an atom whose atomic number is 10 (electronic configuration: 2, 8) and fluoride ion is an ion of fluorine atom. The atomic number of fluorine is 11 (electronic configuration: 2, 8, 1) and it can lose one electron to form fluoride ion whose electronic configuration is 2, 8.

12. Element X has electronic configuration 2, 8, 8, 8, 1. Without identifying X,

(i) Predict the sign and change on a simple ion of X.

(ii) Write whether X will be an oxidising agent or a reducing agent. Why?

Ans. (i) The element X has one electron in its valence shell. So, it can lose one electron. Hence, the sign of simple ion of X is '+ ve' and charge is +1.

(ii) X can lose one electron. So, it is a reducing agent.

13. Give two uses of isotopes.

Ans. Two uses of isotopes are:

(i) Isotope of cobalt $^{60}_{27}Co$ is used in radiotherapy for treating cancer and other diseases.

(ii) $^{14}_{6}C$ is used for determining the age of historical or geographical material.

14. Match the atomic numbers 4, 14, 8, 15 and 19 with each of the following:

(i) A solid non-metal of valency 3.
(ii) A gas of valency 2.
(iii) A metal of valency 1.
(iv) A non-metal of valency 4.

Ans. (i) A solid non-metal of valency 3 is15

(ii) A gas of valency 2 is 8

(iii) A metal of valency 1 is 19

(iv) A non-metal of valency 4 is14

15. Elements X, Y and Z have atomic numbers 6, 9 and 12 respectively. Which one:

(i) forms an anion? (ii) forms a cation? (iii) has four electrons in its valence shell?

Ans. Electronic configuration of X (Atomic number = 6) is 2, 4.

Electronic configuration of Y (Atomic number = 9) is 2, 7

Electronic configuration of Z (Atomic number = 12) is 2, 8, 2

(i) Element that can form anion is Y.

(ii) Element that can form cation is Z.

(iii) Element that has four electrons in its valence shell is X.

16. $^{24}_{12}Mg$ and $^{26}_{12}Mg$ are symbols of two isotopes of magnesium.

(i) Compare the atoms of these isotopes with respect to:

(a) The composition of their nuclei
(b) Their electronic configurations

(ii) Why the two isotopes of magnesium have different mass numbers?

Ans. (i)

For the isotope $^{24}_{12}Mg$, atomic number is 12 and mass number is 24.

Number of neutrons = Mass number – Atomic number

= 24 – 12 = 12

So, number of protons and number of neutron in $^{24}_{12}Mg$ are 12.

For the isotope $^{26}_{12}Mg$, atomic number is 12 and mass number is 26.

Number of neutrons = Mass number – Atomic number

= 26 – 12 = 14

So, In $^{24}_{12}Mg$, number of proton are 12 and number of neutron are 14.

(ii) The two isotopes of magnesium have different mass numbers because both the isotopes contain different number of neutrons.

17. Write down the electronic configuration of the following:

(i) $^{27}_{13}X$ (ii) $^{35}_{17}Y$

Write down the number of electrons in X and neutrons in Y.

Ans. (i) Electronic configuration of X is 2, 8, 3.

(ii) Electronic configuration of Y is 2, 8, 7.

Number of electrons in X is 13

Number of neutrons of Y = Mass number of Y – number. of protons

= 35 – 17 = 18

18. An element A atomic number 7 mass number 14.

B: electronic configuration 2, 8, 8.

C: electrons 13, neutrons 14.

D: protons 18 neutrons 22.

E: electronic configuration 2, 8, 8, 1.

Answer the following:

(i) What is valency of each element? (ii) Which one is metal?

(iii) Which is an non-metal? (iv) Which is inert gas?

Ans. (i)

Element	Valency
A	3
B	0
C	3
D	0
E	1

(ii) Metals are C and E

(iii) Non-metals — A

(iv) Inert gas—B and D

19. In the formation of the compound XY_2, an atom X gives one electrons to each Y atom. What is the nature of bond in XY_2? Draw the electron dot structure of this compound.

Ans. The X atom gives one electrons to each Y atom. So, the nature of bond in XY_2 is electrovalent bond.

The electron dot structure of the compound XY_2 is:

$$X: + 2Y \longrightarrow X^{2+} \ 2Y^{-}$$

20. What is the drawback of Rutherford's model of atom?

Ans. According to the classical laws of mechanics and electrodynamics, if an electrically charged particle is in motion, it inevitably radiates energy. Thus, an electron on moving around the nucleus continuously, then electron should radiate energy, *i.e.*, loses energy. As a result, it should be gradually pulled towards the nucleus and end up colliding with it. This should result in the total collapse of the atom. If it was so, the atom should be highly unstable and hence matter would not exist in the form that we know. Also we know that a atom is structurally stable. Thus, Rutherford's model failed to explain the stability of an atom.

21. What are main postulates of Dalton's atomic theory?

Ans. Main postulates of Dalton's atomic theory are:

(i) Matter consists of very small and indivisible particles called atoms.

(ii) Atoms can neither be created nor be destroyed.

(iii) The atoms of an element are alike in all respects but they differ from the atoms of other elements.

(iv) Atoms of an element combine in small numbers to form molecules.

22. An atom of an element X has 3 electrons in its third shell. **[November, 2019]**

(i) State its electronic configuration.

(ii) State the number of protons in one atom of X.

(iii) It the mass number of X is 27, how many neutrons are present in one atom of X?

Ans. (i) As the element X has 3 shells and there are 3 electrons in third shell, it has electronic configuration of 2, 8, 3.

(ii) The total number of electrons in the given atom is 2 + 8 + 3 = 13. Hence, the number of protons in element X are also 13.

(iii) Number of neutrons is given by:

Number of neutrons = Mass number – Number of protons

= 27 – 13 = 14

Hence, number of neutrons in element X are 14.

Chapter 5. The Periodic Table

1. How are cations and anions formed?

Ans. Metals lose electrons to form positively charged particles called cations whereas non-metals gains electrons to form negatively charged particles called anions.

2. What is modern periodic law?

Ans. According to modern periodic law, physical and chemical properties of elements are the periodic function of their atomic numbers.

3. Define bridge elements.

Ans. Elements of second period show resemblance in properties with elements of the next group of the third period, leading to diagonal relationship. Such elements are called bridge elements. For example, Lithium (Li) and Magnesium (Mg), etc.

4. What is periodicity of elements?

Ans. **The** properties that reappear at regular intervals, or in which there is gradual variation, *i.e.*, increase or decrease at regular intervals are called periodic properties and the phenomenon is known as periodicity of elements.

5. Arrange the following elements in increasing order of atomic size. Also give reason for your answer. Lithium, Carbon, Fluorine, Nitrogen.

Ans. Moving along a period size of atoms decrease. So, Fluorine < Nitrogen < Carbon< Lithium.

6. Arrange the following halogens in decreasing order of reactivity. Give reason. Iodine, fluorine , Chlorine, Bromine.

Ans. Down the group reactivity decreases. So, Fluorine > Chlorine > Bromine > Iodine

7. What is meant in the periodic table by:

(i) A group, and (ii) A period?

Ans. (i) In periodic table, the vertical columns are called group.

(ii) In periodic table, the horizontal rows are called period.

8. Why alkali metals are good reducing agents?

Ans. Alkali metals have greater tendency to lose or donate electrons which make them good reducing agents.

9. "Hydrogen occupies a unique position in the modern periodic table". Justify the statement.

Ans. In electronic configuration, hydrogen resembles with alkali metals. Moreover, it combines with halogen, oxygen and sulphur to give similar type of compounds as given by alkali metals. e.g. (HCl, NaCl), (H_2O, Na_2O), (H_2S, Na_2S).

But just like halogens, it exists in diatomic form and combines with metals and non-metals to form covalent compounds. In this periodic table, a unique position has been given to the hydrogen. It is kept and the top left corner because of its unique characteristic.

10. How many elements are present in:

(i) First period? (ii) Second period? (iii) Third period?

Ans. (i) 2 elements (ii) 8 elements (iii) 8 elements.

11. (i) In a group where do you expect to find the most metallic element?

(ii) In a group where do you expect to find the element having maximum size?

(iii) In which group lanthanoids and actinoids are present?

Ans. (i) At the bottom. (ii) At the bottom (iii) Group 3.

12. What is the reaction of alkali metals with:

(i) Air, (ii) water and (iii) acid?

Ans. (i) Alkali metals react rapidly with oxygen and water vapour in the air.

$$4Na + O_2 \rightarrow 2Na_2O$$

(ii) Alkali metals react violently with water and produce hydrogen.

$$2Na + 2H_2O \rightarrow 2NaOH + H_2$$

(iii) Alkali metals react violently with dilute HCl and dilute H_2SO_4 to produce hydrogen.

$$2Na + 2HCl \rightarrow 2NaCl + H_2$$

13. Element P has atomic number 19. To which group and period does P belong? Is it a metal or non-metal? Explain.

Ans. Electronic configuration of P is 2, 8, 8, 1

Valency of P is one therefore, it belongs to group IA.

Number of electron shells in a given element is equal to the number of period to which it belongs. Here, number of shell is four. Therefore, it belongs to period 4.

P is metal.

14. Write the electronic configuration of the first two alkaline earth metals.

Ans. Electronic configuration of first two alkaline earth metal is:

Berellium (Be) = 2, 2

Magnesium (Mg) = 2, 8, 2

15. Lithium, sodium and potassium elements were put in one group on the basis of their similar properties. What are those properties?

Ans. The similar properties of lithium, sodium and potassium are:

(i) They have one electron in outermost shell.

(ii) They form unipositive ions.

(iii) They are good reducing agents.

(iv) All these are soft metals.

(v) All these metals impart colour to flame.

16. The electronic configuration of an element is $^{39}_{19}X$.

(i) In which period and group the element X present?

(ii) What is the number of protons and neutrons in X?

(iii) Is X metal or non-metal?

(iv) Write the electronic configuration of X.

Ans. (i) Group-1 and period -4

(ii) Number of protons in X is 19 and mass number is 39. So,

Number of neutrons = 39 – 19 = 20

(iii) As the element X is present in Group 1, it is a metal.

(iv) Atomic number of X is 19. So, electronic configuration is 2, 8, 8, 1.

17. What is the need for classification of elements?

Ans. Following are the reasons for classification of elements:

(i) Classification helps in studying the elements in organised manner.

(ii) Classification helps in correlating the properites of elements with fundamental properites of all states of matter.

(iii) It helps in defining the relationship of one element with other.

18. (i) What happens to the basic character of oxides when we move down the group?

(ii) What happens to the acidic character of elements in a period?

Ans. (i) As we move down the group, the basic character of oxides increases.

(ii) As we move across the period, the acidic character of oxides increases.

19. (i) What is/are the valency/valencies of metal?

(ii) Inert gases have zero valency. Why?

Ans. (i) Valency of metals are 1, 2 or 3.

(ii) Inert gases have zero valency as they can neither lose electron nor they can gair they have complete octet (except helium which has complete duplet).

20. A metal M forms and oxide having the formula, MO. It belongs to 2nd period in the modern periodic table. Write its atomic number and valency.

Ans. Since, the metal form MO type oxide, it belongs to second group and has configuration 2, 2 because metal M have two shells. Thus, atomic number of the element are 4 and its valency is 2.

21. Two elements R and S present in same period and in Group 17 and 18 respectively. Compare the following characteristics.

(i) Number of electrons in both the elements

(ii) Their tendency to form compounds

(iii) Their valency

(iv) Their ability to form ions

Ans. (i) As element R is present in group 17 and S is present in group 18. S has one more electron than R.

(ii) R is present in group 17, *i.e.,* halogen group and S is present in group 18, *i.e.,* inert gas. So, R can form compounds but S cannot.

(iii) R has valency one and S has valency zero.

(iv) R can easily form negative ions by gaining one electron but S cannot form ions as it has stable configuration.

22. Sodium and aluminium have atomic number 11 and 13, respectively. They are separated by one element in the periodic table and have valencies 1 and 3 repsectively. Chlorine and potassium are also separated by one elements in the periodic table (their atomic numbers being 17 and 19, repsectively) and yet both have valency 1. Explain.

Ans. Electronic configuration of Na is 2, 8, 1.

Electronic configuration of Al is 2, 8, 3.

Sodium and aluminium both have 1 and 3 electrons in their valence shell. Therefore, they exhibits valency 1 and 3 respectively.

Electronic configuration of Chlorine (Cl) is 2, 8, 7.

Electronic configuration Potassium (K) is 2, 8, 8, 1.

Chlorine wants one electron to possess stable electronic configuration of nearest noble gas. So, it exhibits valency 1. Again, potassium can lose one electron to possess stable electronic configuration of nearest noble gas. Hence, its valency is 1.

23. (i) Name the first three alkaline earth metals.

(ii) What is the name given to group 17 elements?

Ans. (i) First three alkaline earth metals are berrylium , magnesium and calcium.

(ii) The name given to group 17 elements is halogen.

24. (i) Name the period which is the longest one.

(ii) Why group 17 elements are highly reactive?

Ans. (i) Period 6 is the longest period.

(ii) Group 17 elements are highly reactive because they have incomplete valence shells. They need only one electron to complete the octet.

25. Match the atomic number 4, 6, 11, 15 and 18 with each of the following: **[February, 2020]**

(i) A solid non-metal of velency 3.

(ii) A gas belonging to zero group.

(iii) An element with 2 electrons in the valence shell.

(iv) A non-metal of valency 4.

(v) A metal with one electron in the third shell.

Ans. (i) A solid non-metal of valency 3 =15

(ii) A gas belonging to zero group = 18

(iii) An element with 2 electrons in the valence shell = 4

(iv) A non-metal of valency four = 6

(v) A metal with one electron in the third shell = 11

26. An atom of an element is represented as $^{24}_{12}A$. **[February, 2020]**

(i) Write the number of protons present in one atom of the element.

(ii) Write its electronic configuration.

(iii) State whether it is a metal or a non-metal.

Ans. (i) No. of protons = 12

(ii) Electronic configuration K: L: M: [2, 8, 2]

(iii) This is a metal.

27. How do the alkaline earth metals occur in nature?

Ans. Alkaline earth metals are reactive metals (less reactive than alkali metals). Hence, they do not occur in free state in nature.

28. Arrange the following elements in the increasing order of their atomic radii.

(i) Li, Be, F, N (ii) Cl, At, Br, I

Ans. (i) F < N < Be < Li (ii) Cl < Br < I < At

29. Compare the radii of two species X and Y. Give reasons.

(i) X has 12 protons and 12 electrons (ii) Y has 12 protons and 10 electrons

Ans. The radii of species Y will be smaller than species X because Y is formed when X loses 2 electrons. Hence, Y is the cation and protons are more than electrons in Y, so electrons are strongly attracted by the nucleus and are pulled inward. Hence, the size decreases.

30. Write a reaction of alkaline earth metal with:

(i) Oxygen (ii) Water

Ans. (i) Alkaline earth metals reacts with oxygen to form respective oxides.

$$2M + O_2 \longrightarrow 2\,MO$$

(where, M = any alkaline earth metals)

(ii) They reacts with water to produce alkali hydroxide and hydrogen gas

$$\underset{\text{Alkaline earthmetal}}{M} + 2H_2O \rightarrow \underset{\text{Alkali hydroxide}}{M(OH)_2} + H_2 \uparrow$$

31. Give one use of (i) argon gas (ii) neon gas.

Ans. (i) Argon gas because of its inert nature is used to provide an inert atmosphere in high temperature metallurgical process.

(ii) Neon gas is used in discharge tubes.

32. What was Mendeleev's basis for classification of elements?

Ans. Mendeleev's basis for classification of elements are as follows:

(i) Similarities in the chemical properties of elements.

(ii) Increasing order of atomic weights of elements.

(iii) Periodicity of properties of elements.

33. Name the following: **[November, 2019]**

(i) An alkali metal in period 3. (ii) A halogen in period 2.

(iii) The noble gas with three shells. (iv) The non-metal of period 3 which has valency 2.

Ans. (i) An alkali metal in period 3 – Sodium (Na).

(ii) A halogen in period 2 – Fluorine (F).

(iii) The noble gas with three shells – Argon (Ar).

(iv) The non-metal of period 3 which has valency 2 – Sulphur (S).

34. What are the characteristics of long form of periodic table?

Ans. The different characteristics of the long form of the periodic table are given below:

(i) The highly metallic elements are placed on the left hand side of the period.

(ii) The highly non-metallic elements are placed on the right hand side of the

(iii) The transition elements are accommodated between metals and non-metals.

(iv) The noble gases are placed in group 18.

(v) The elements present in the left and right side of the veritical columns a elements or representative elements. The elements having complete penu called normal elements or the representative elements.

(vi) Lanthanoids and Actinoids are placed outside the main body of the period.

35. Mendeleev predicted the existence of certain elements not known at that time and named two of them as eka-silicon and eka-aluminium.

(i) Which elements have taken the place of these elements?

(ii) Mention the group and the period of these elements in the modern periodic table.

(iii) Classify these elements as metals or non-metals or metalloids.

(iv) How many valence electrons are present in each one of them.

Ans. (i) Germanium and gallium have taken the place of these elements.

(ii) Germanium — Group 14, Period 4
Gallium — Group 13, Period 4

(iii) They are metalloids.

(iv) In germanium, the number of valence electrons are 4 and in gallium valence electrons are 3.

36. How are the electrons distributed in different orbits (shells)?

Ans. The electrons are distributed in different orbits in the following ways:

(i) The maximum number of electrons present in a shell is given by the formula $2n^2$, where n is the orbit number or energy level, 1, 2, 3........ .
Therefore, the maximum number of electrons in different shells are as follow:
First orbit or K-shell $= 2 \times 1^2 = 2$
Second orbit or L-shell $= 2 \times 2^2 = 8$
Third orbit or M-shell $= 2 \times 3^2 = 18$
Fourth orbit or N-shell $= 2 \times 4^2 = 32$ and so on.

(ii) The maximum number of electrons that can be accommodated in the outermost orbit are 8.

(iii) The penultimate shell (*i.e.*, the second last shell) cannot accommodat more than 18 electrons.

(iv) The anti-penultimate shell (*i.e.*, the third last shell) can have maximum of 32 electrons.

(v) Electrons are not accommodated in a given shell, unless the inner shells are filled *i.e.*, the shells are filled in a stepwise manner.

37. Elements have been arranged in the following sequence on the basis of their increasing atomic masses.

F, Na, Mg, Al, Si, P, S, Cl, Ar, K

(i) Which two sets of elements which have similar properties?

(ii) Which law of classification of elements is represented by the following sequence?

Ans. (i) The elements are arranged in the order of increasing atomic masses, so according to Newland's law of octaves there was a repeatition of properties in every eighth element as compared to the given element.
The two sets of elements which have similar properties are:

Set I → F, Cl Set II → Na, K

(ii) Newland's law of Octaves is represented by the given sequence.

Chapter 6. Hydrogen

1. Complete the following reactions.
   (i) Sodium hydroxide + Zinc → Hydrogen + ____________
   (ii) Calcium + water → Calcium hydroxide + ____________

Ans. (i) Sodium hydroxide + Zinc → Hydrogen + Sodium zincate
(ii) Calcium + water → Calcium hydroxide + Hydrogen

2. Name the gas evolves when calcium reacts with water.

Ans. Hydrogen

3. What is the nature of solutions of metal hydroxides of sodium, potassium and calcium?

Ans. The nature of solutions of metal hydroxides of sodium, potassium and calcium turn red litmus blue showing their alkaline nature.

4. What do you mean by amphoteric nature of elements?

Ans. Amphoteric compounds aere those compounds that can react with both acids and bases. For example oxides and hydroxides of zinc, lead and aluminium.

5. Arrange the following metals in order of increasing reactivity.

Ans. Potassium > Calcium > Magnesium > Hydrogen
Hydrogen, potassium, calcium, magnesium.

6. Name one method of manufacture of hydrogen.

Ans. Bosch Process

7. Write the chemical reactions involved in Bosch process.

Ans. Manufacture of hydrogen by Bosch process consists of two steps:
Step 1: Steam is passed over hot coke (1000°C) in furnaces of a special design, called converters giving water gas.

$$\underbrace{C}_{\text{Coke}} + \underbrace{H_2O}_{\text{Steam}} \xrightarrow[\Delta]{1000°C} \underbrace{(CO + H_2)}_{\text{Water gas}}$$

Step 2: Water gas is mixed with excess steam and passed over heated ferric oxide which acts as a catalyst and chormic oxide Cr_2O_3 which acts as a promoter.

$$\underbrace{(CO + H_2)}_{\text{Water gas}} + \underbrace{H_2O}_{\text{Steam}} \xrightarrow[450°C]{Fe_2O_3} Co_2 + 2H_2 +$$

This reaction is exothermic in nature.

8. Give one method of removal of carbon dioxide from the mixture of carbon dioxide and hydrogen.

Ans. The carbon dioxide can be removed from the mixture by passing it through caustic potash solution which removes carbon dioxide by reacting with it, leaving hydrogen.

$$2KOH + CO_2 \rightarrow K_2CO_3 + H_2O$$

9. How magnesium reacts with boiling water?

Ans. Magnesium reacts slowly with boiling water and forms a base, magnesium hydroxide liberating hydrogen gas.

$$Mg + 2H_2O \rightarrow Mg(OH)_2 + H_2\uparrow$$

10. What happens when steam is passed to red hot coke?

Ans. When steam is passed over red hot coke, water gas $(CO + H_2)$ is formed.

$$C + H_2O \xrightarrow{1270\ K} \underbrace{CO + H_2}_{\text{Water gas}}$$

11. Name an isotope of hydrogen which:
    (i) has same number of proton and neutron

(ii) is most abundant on Earth

Ans. (i) Deuterium (^2_1D or ^2_1H)

(ii) Protium (^1_1H) – 99.98%.

12. What is the purpose of oxyhydrogen flame?

Ans. It is used for welding and cutting of metals.

13. Name two metals, which can displace hydrogen from acid as well as alkali.

Ans. Aluminium and zinc.

14. Why magnesium is not used in laboratory production of hydrogen?

Ans. Magnesium is expensive metal. So, it is not used in production of hydrogen.

15. Which solution is used to remove arsine and phosphine from the mixture of hydrogen?

Ans. Silver nitrate solution is used to remove arsine and phosphine from the mixture of hydrogen.

16. Why is hydrogen called as 'inflammable air'?

Ans. Hydrogen is called inflammable air because of its combustible nature.

17. Why is hot concentrated sulphuric acid not used in the preparation of hydrogen?

Ans. Hot concentrated sulphuric acid is not used in preparation of hydrogen gas as it is a strong oxidiser and will produce sulphur dioxide.

$$Zn + 2H_2SO_4 \rightarrow ZnSO_4 + SO_2 + 2H_2O$$

18. Hydrogen can be prepared with the help of cold water. Give a reaction of hydrogen with:

(i) A monovalent metal (ii) A divalent metal

Ans. (i) A monovalent metal

$2K + H_2 \xrightarrow{\varnothing} 2KH$

(ii) A divalent metal

$Ca + H_2 \xrightarrow{\varnothing} CaH_2$

19. State whether the following conversions are oxidation or reduction reactions.

(i) $Cu^{2+} + 2e^- \rightarrow Cu$ (ii) $K \rightarrow K^+ + e^-$

Ans. (i) Reduction reaction

(ii) Oxidation reaction

20. In the following reaction write half reactions for this reaction and name the:

(i) Oxidising agent (ii) Substance oxidised (iii) Reducing agent

Ans. Oxidation half reaction: $B \rightarrow B^+ + e^-$

Reduction half reaction: $A^+ + e^- \rightarrow A$

(i) Oxidising agent is A.

(ii) Substance oxidised is B.

(iii) Reducing agent is B.

21. Hydrogen is evolved when dilute HCl reacts with magnesium, but nothing happens in case of mercury and silver. Explain.

Ans. Hydrogen is evolved when dilute HCl reacts with magnesium, but nothing happens in case of mercury and silver because mercury and silver are less reactive than hydrogen.

22. Which metal is preferred for preparation of hydrogen:

(i) from water and (ii) from Acid?

Ans. (i) Magnesium

(ii) Zinc

23. (i) Name the impurities present in hydrogen prepared in the laboratory.

(ii) Why nitric acid is not used in preparation of hydrogen?

Ans. (i) The impurities present in hydrogen prepared in the laboratory are hydrogen sulphide, sulphur dioxide, phosphine, arsine, carbon dioxide, etc.

(ii) Nitric acid is not used in preparation of hydrogen because it is a powerful oxidising agent and the oxygen formed due to its decomposition oxidises the hydrogen to give water, thus defeating the purpose of the reaction.

24. (i) Write the equation for the laboratory preparation of hydrogen. **[February, 2020]**

(ii) How is the gas collected?

(iii) Write the confirmatory test for Hydrogen.

Ans. (i) Laboratory preparation of hydrogen: In the laboratory, hydrogen is prepared by the action of zinc on dilute sulphuric acid where zinc sulphate is obtained along with the evolution of the hydrogen gas.

$$Zn\ (s) + dil.H_2SO_4(l) \longrightarrow ZnSO_4\ (s) + H_2\ (g)$$

(ii) Hydrogen gas generated is collected by downward displacement of water as it is insoluble in water and cannot be collected by downward displacement of air as it forms an explosive mixture with air.

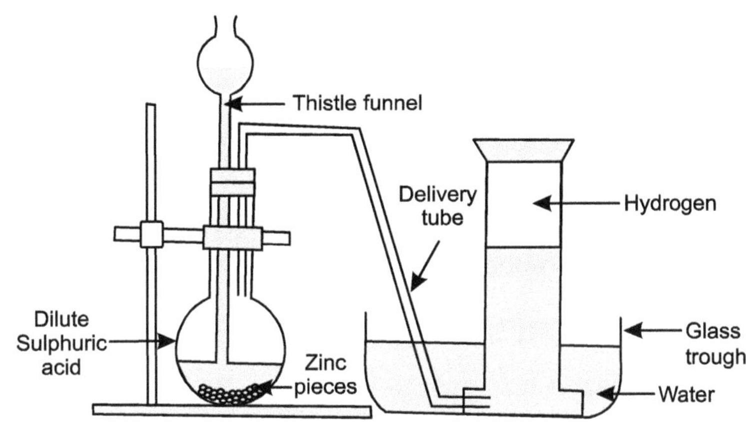

Preparation of Hydrogen gas

(iii) A lighted splint is used for the confirmatory test of hydrogen. Hydrogen gas burns with a 'pop' sound and extinguishes the lighted splint, confirming the presence of hydrogen gas. Also it burns silently in air or oxygen with a pale blue flame forming water.

$$2H_2 + O_2 \longrightarrow H_2O$$

25. (i) Name the industrial method by which hydrogen can be prepared on a large scale. **[November, 2019]**

(ii) Give the two relevant equations involved in the above method.

(iii) How is carbon dioxide removed from the mixture of carbon dioxide and hydrogen?

Ans. (i) Hydrogen gas can be prepared on a large scale by reaction of steam on hydrocarbons or coke at high temperatures in the presence of catalyst. The process in named as Bosch process.

(ii) The two relevant equations involved in the above method are:

$$C(s) + H_2O\ (g) \xrightarrow{1270k} CO\ (g) + H_2\ (g)$$

$$CO(g) + H_2O\ (g) \rightarrow CO_2\ (g) + H_2(g)$$

(iii) Carbon dioxide can be removed from the mixture of carbon dioxide and hydrogen by scrubbing with sodium arsentite solution.

26. How is hydrogen obtained from:

(i) dilute sulphric acid, (ii) sodium hydroxide and (iii) water?

Give one equation in each case.

Ans. (i) When metal reacts with dilute sulphuric acid, hydrogen is obtained along with metal salts.

$$Mg(s) + H_2SO_4\ (aq) \longrightarrow MgSO_4(aq) + H_2(g)$$

(ii) When zinc reacts with sodium hydroxide, sodium zincate is formed and hydrogen gas is evolved.

$$Zn(s) + 2NaOH(aq) \longrightarrow Na_2ZnO_2(aq) + H_2\ (g)$$

(iii) When acidified water is electrolysed using platinum electrodes, hydrogen gas is evolved at cathode.

$$H_2O \longrightarrow H^+(aq) + OH^-(aq)$$

At cathode: $2H+ + 2e^- \longrightarrow 2\,H \longrightarrow H_2$

At anode: $OH^-\ (aq) \longrightarrow OH + e^-$

$$4OH + 4\,e^- \longrightarrow 2H_2O + O_2$$

27. (i) Explain the industrial applications of hydrogen depending on the heat liberated when its atoms combine on the surface of a metal.

(ii) Give the difference between oxidation and reduction with examples.

Ans. (i) Due to the property of heat liberation on combining atoms of hydrogen on the surface of the metal, hydrogen is used in atomic hydrogen torch for welding/cutting.

(ii) Oxidation is defined as a chemical process which involves either the addition of oxygen to the substance or loss of hydrogen from the substance.

For example:

(a) Oxidation

$$H_2S + Cl_2 \longrightarrow 2HCl + S$$

(b) Oxidation

$$2Cu + O_2 \longrightarrow 2CuO$$

Reduction is defined as a chemical process which involves either the addition of hydrogen to the substance or loss of oxygen from the substance.

For example:

Reduction

$$2Na + H_2 \longrightarrow 2NaH$$

Reduction

$$ZnO + H_2 \longrightarrow Zn + H_2O$$

28. Why is it safe to store acid in a copper container but not to store in an iron container?

Ans. Iron is placed above hydrogen in the activity series, hence it displaces hydrogen from an acid when the acid is kept in an iron container.

$$Fe + H_2SO_4 \longrightarrow FeSO_4 + H_2\uparrow$$

In this process iron corrodes and hence, wall of container deplete.

On the other side, copper is less reactive than hydrogen, hence it cannot react with acid to displace hydrogen.

$$Cu + H_2SO_4 \longrightarrow \text{No reaction}$$

And thus, the copper container remains harmless.

29. Justify the position of hydrogen in the periodic table on the basis of its electronic configuration.

The electronic configuration of hydrogen can be compared as follows

Ans. (i) The electronic configuration of hydrogen ($1s^1$) is similar to the outer electronic configuration of alkali metals, which is ns^1.

Element with electronic configuration	K L M
Hydrogen (H)	1
Lithium (li)	2, 1
Sodium (Na)	2, 8, 1

(ii) Like halogens, hydrogen requires only one electron to achieve the nearest inert or noble gas configuration.*e.g.*,

H $\left(\begin{smallmatrix}k\\1\end{smallmatrix}\right)$ has one electron less than He $\left(\begin{smallmatrix}k\\2\end{smallmatrix}\right)$

F $\left(\begin{smallmatrix}k & L\\2 & 7\end{smallmatrix}\right)$ has one electron less than Ne $\left(\begin{smallmatrix}k & L\\2 & 8\end{smallmatrix}\right)$

Cl $\left(\begin{smallmatrix}k & L & M\\2 & 8 & 7\end{smallmatrix}\right)$ has one electron less than Ar $\left(\begin{smallmatrix}k & L & M\\2 & 8 & 8\end{smallmatrix}\right)$

As we can see hydrogen resembles with both the alkali metal group and the halogen group. This arises confusion about the placing of it in the periodic table. But considering its electronic. configuration and fact that it has one valence electron like alkali metals it has been palced in the group-I of the periodic table.

Chapter 7. Study of Gas Laws

1. Give mathematical expression of Boyle's law.

Ans. Boyle's law equation is, $P_1V_1 = P_2V_2$.

2. Convert 20°C to Kelvin.

Ans. As, 20°C = 20 + 273
= 293 K

3. Why it is necessary to compare gases at S.T.P.

Ans. The volume of a given mass of enclosed dry gas depends on the pressure of the gas and the temperature of the gas in Kelvin. So, to express the volume of gases we need to compare theses at STP.

4. Hot air is filled into balloons used for meteorological purposes. Explain.

Ans. Volume of a given mass of gas is directly proportional to its temperature, hence density decreases with an increases in temperature. This is the reason why hot air is filled into balloons used for meteorological purposes.

5. What is the standard temperature and pressure?

Ans. Standard temperature is 0°C or 273 K and standard pressure is 1 atmospheric unit or 760 mm Hg.

6. What is the relationship between °C and K?

Ans. The value on the Celsius scale can be converted to Kelvin scale by adding 273 to it.
For example; 35°C can be converted into Kelvin as follows:
35°C = 35 + 273
= 308 K

7. What is the advantage of Kelvin scale?

Ans. The advantage of Kelvin scale is that it makes application and use of gas laws simple. Even more singificantly as all values on Kelvin scale are positive.

8. Increase of volume occurs when pressure is decreased. Explain.

Ans. Gases increase in volume on decreasing pressure and increasing temperature. When pressure on an enclosed gas is reduced, it particles move apart thus, increasing their intermolecular spaces. As a result volume of the gas increases.

9. During the preparation of hydrogen sulphide gas for practical, the smell of the gas spreads in the whole room. Name the phenomenon.

Ans. The phenomenon is diffusion.

10. (i) How can you define the gas?
(ii) Give some characteristic properties of gases.
(iii) What are the factors upon which the behaviour of gases do not depend?

Ans. (i) Gas is state of matter which has definite mass but have neither definite volume.
(ii) Some characteristic properties of gases are:
(a) They have neither a fixed volume nor a fixed shape.
(b)They exert pressure in all directions
(c)They are highly compressible
(d) They are highly expansible.
(iii) The behavior of gases do not depend upon chemical nature or colour or odour.

11. How is molecular motion related to temperature?

Ans. As the temperature increases, molecular motion increases and when temperature decreases, molecular motion decreases. This is variation due to vibrations or change in kinetic energy of molecules due to the effect of temperature.

12. Give some standard variables for gas laws.

Ans. The physical behaviour of gases can be described by three standard variables, that is, Volume (V), Pressure (P) and temperature (T).

13. What is the relationship between Celsius and Kelvin scale of temperature?

Ans. The relationship between Celsius and Kelvin scale of temperate is K = °C + 273.

14. Inflating a balloon seems to violate Boyle's law. Explain.

Ans. According to Boyle's law, on increasing pressure volume decreases. When air is blown into a balloon volume and pressure inside the balloon increases. So, Boyle's law is violated.

15. One of the assumptions of kinetic theory of gases states that "there is no force of attraction between the molecules of a gas." How far is this statement correct? Is it possible to liquiefy an ideal gas? Explain.

Ans. This statement is correct only for ideal gases. It is not possible to liquefy an ideal gas because there is no intermolecular forces of attractions between the molecules of an ideal gas.

16. One of the assumptions of kinetic theory of gases is that there is no force of attraction between the molecules of a gas. State and explain the evidence that shows that the assumption is not applicable for real gas.

Ans. Real gases can be liquefied by cooling and compression of the gas. This proves that forces of attraction exist among the molecules.

17. Write the value of:

(i) Standard pressure in:

(a) mm of Hg (b) cm of Hg

(c) atm (d) torr

(ii) Standard temperature in:

(a) °C (b) K

Ans. (i) Standard pressure

(a) 760 mm of Hg (b) 76 cm of Hg

(c) 1 atmosphere (d) 760 torr

(ii) Standard temperature

(a) 0°C (b) 273 + 0°C = 273 K

18. Boyle's law states that at constant temperature, if pressure is increased on a gas, volume decreases and vice-versa. But when we fill air in a balloon, volume as well as pressure increase. Why?

Ans. The law is applicable only for a definite mass of the gas. As we fill air into the ballon, we are introducing more and more air into the balloon.

19. Whenever there is experiment in the laboratory, hydrogen sulphide gas (offensive odour) is prepared for some test. There is smell of the gas which we can observe 50 metres away. Name the phenomenon.

Ans. This is because of the mixing of hydrogen sulphide gas with air. This property is called diffusion. It is because, gas molecules are always in random motion and there are large vacant spaces between the molecules of a gas.

20. The molecular theory accounts for the pressure exerted by a gas in a closed vessel as a result of the gas molecules striking on the walls of the vessel. How will the pressure change, if:

(i) the volume is made half of original value, maintaining the temperature constant?

(ii) temperature is doubled maintaining the volume constant?

Ans. (i) When the volume is halved, the number of gas molecules striking per unit area of the walls of the vessel is doubled. Thus, the pressure is doubled.

(ii) When the temperature is doubled, the average kinetic energy of the gas molecules gets doubled. Thus, the pressure is also doubled.

21. In terms of Charles' law explain why –273°C is the lowest possible temperature?

Ans. According to Charles' law, $V_t = V_0\left[1+\frac{t}{273}\right]$

At $t = -273°C$, $V_t = V_0\left[1-\frac{273}{273}\right] = 0$

22. While stating the volume of a gas, the temperature and pressure should also be given. Why?

Ans. The volume of a fixed mass of agas depends upon the temperature as well as pressure. Thus, while stating the volume of a gas, the temperature and pressure should be specified.

23. The product of pressure and volume of an enclosed dry gas at a given temperature is always a constant quantity. Explain.

Short Answer Type Questions

Ans. According to Boyle's law, temperature remaining constant, volume of a fixed mass of a dry gas is inversely proportional to the pressure exerted on it.F

Mathematically, $V \propto \frac{1}{p}$ (T is kept constant)

where, V is the volume of a certain mass of a gas at pressure p and temperature T.

$\therefore\ V = \frac{k}{p}$ (where, k is a constant of proportionality)

$\therefore$ pV = k

Thus, the product of pressure and volume of an enclosed dry gas at a given temperature is always a constant quantity.

24. How did Charles' law state the concept of absolute scale of temperature?

Ans. From the Charles' law, at constant pressure, the volume of a given mass of a gas increases or decreases by $\frac{1}{273}$ of its volume at 0°C for each 1°C rise or fall in temperature.

Suppose V_0 be the volume of a fixed mass of a gas at 0°C and its pressure is p.

$\therefore$ At constant pressure, volume of gas (V) at t°C is

$$V = V_0 + \frac{1}{273} \times V_0 t$$

Volume of a gas at –373°C (at constant pressure),

$$V_{-273°C} = V_0 + \frac{1}{273} \times V_0(-273)$$
$$= V_0 - V_0 = 0$$

The temperature, – 273°C is called absolute zero.

25. State the laws which are represented by the given graphs.

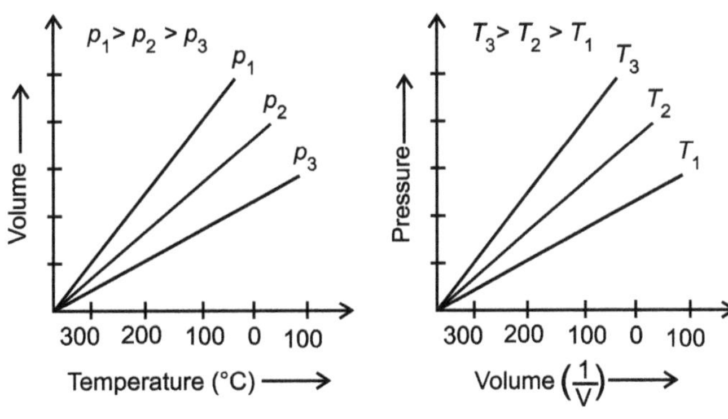

Ans. (i) Charles' law $V \propto T$ (n, p constant)

(ii) Boyle's law $p \propto \frac{1}{V}$

26. (i) What does STP or NTP denote?

(ii) Why is it necessary to compare gases at STP?

Ans. (i) STP stands for standard temperature temperature and normal pressure.

(ii) The volume of a fixed mass of dry enclosed gas depends upon the pressure of the gas and temperature of the gas in Kelvin, hence to express the volume the gases, we need to compare these to STP.

27. Explain, why

(i) temperature – 273°C is a theoretical temperature but cannot be achieved?

(ii) Kelvin temperature is always positive?

Ans. (i) At –273°C, volume of a gas becomes zero . But it is not possible because gas is a state of matter and cannot have zero volume. Thus, –273°C is a theortical temperature, which cannot be achieved.

(ii) Kelvin scale of temperature starts from zero, which is equal to –273°C . Temperature below –273°C not possible. Thus, Kelvin temperature is alwa positive.

28. (i) Define Charles' Law. **[November, 2019]**

(ii) What is meant by standard temperature and pressure? **[November, 2019]**

Ans. (i) Charles' law states that the volume of a given amount of gas is directly proportional to the absolute (Kelvin) when the pressure is kept constant.

(ii) The standard temperature is 273 K (0° Celsius) and the standard pressure is 1 atm pressure. At standard temperature and pressure (STP), one mole of gas occupies 22.4 L of volume (molar volume).

Chapter 8. Atmospheric Pollution

1. Name the gaseous pollutant that damages the nervous and digestive system and can cause cancer.

Ans. Lead

2. Name the poisonous gas that has chlorine like smell.

Ans. Ozone

3. What is global warming?

Ans. Rise in average temperature of the earth's surface is called global warming.

4. Define green house effect.

Ans. Heating of the earth and its environment due to solar radiation trapped by carbon dioxide and water vapour in the atmosphere is called green house effect.

5. What is the pH of normal rain?

Ans. Normal rain has a pH of 5.6.

6. What are the components of clean and dry air?

Ans. Standard dry air which is mainly composed of three gases: nitrogen, oxygen and argon.

7. Write the reactions that lead to the formation of nitric acid.

Ans. 1st step is combination of nitrogen and oxygen in the presence of thunder and lightning.

$$N_2 + O_2 \xrightarrow[3000YC]{\text{High temperature}} 2NO$$

2nd stpe is oxidation of nitrogen oxide to nitrogen dioxide in the atmosphere.

$$2NO + O_2 \rightarrow 2NO_2$$

3rd step is combination of nitrogen dioxide with water to form a mixture of nitrous acid and nitric acid.

$$2NO_2 + H_2O \rightarrow \underbrace{HNO_2}_{\text{Nitrous acid}} + \underbrace{HNO_3}_{\text{Nitric acid}}$$

8. Write some impact of acid rain.

Ans. Some impacts of acid rain are:

(i) It affects soil chemistry. It removes calcium and potassium which are basic ingredients of soil and thus make the soil less fertile.

(ii) It causes extensive damage to building and sculptural materials like marble, limestone, slate, mortar, etc. These materials become pitted and thus weaken mechanically.

9. How the impact of acid rain can be reduced?

Ans. The impact of acid rain can be reduced by checking the root cause of acid rain, *i.e.*, by reducing the emission of oxides of sulphur and nitrogen. This can be done by using coal or oil with low sulphur content.

10. Write the reaction of formation of ozone.

Ans. 1st step is break down of oxygen molecule by UV radiation.

$$O_2 + UV \rightarrow O + O$$

2nd step is reaction of oxygen atom with oxygen molecule to form ozone.

$$O + O_2 \rightarrow O_3$$

Net reaction is $3O_2 + UV \rightarrow 2O_3$.

11. Give some harmful effects of ozone.

Ans. Some harmful effects of ozone are:

(i) It causes respiratory problems.

(ii) It damages plants and trees.

12. What is the advantage of green house effect?

Ans. Green house effect has played an important role in the evolution of life on earth. Without the green house gases, all the heat coming from the sun would have escaped from the earth, which would then becomes as cold and barren as the moon.

13. What is smog?

Ans. A pollutant, which is a combination oxides of nitrogen and sulphur and of partially oxidized hydrocarbons and their derivatives produced by industries and automobiles forms a dark, dust and soot laden fog and is known as smog.

14. What are the harmful effects of smog?

Ans. Smog is noxious and irritating. It reduces visibility, induces respiratory troubles, can cause death by suffocation.

15. (i) Define atmosphere.

(ii) What are the two forms of oxygen found in the atmosphere?

(iii) Green plants use carbon dioxide for photosynthesis and return oxygen to the atmosphere, even then carbon dioxide is considered to be responsible for green house effect. Explain why?

Ans. (i) The gaseous envelope surrounding the earth is called atmosphere.

(ii) The two forms of oxygen found in the atmosphere are:

(a) Elemental Oxygen: It is normally found in the form of diatomic molecule (O_2) in the lower part of atmosphere. It constitutes about 20.95% of the atmosphere and is non-poisonous.

(b) Ozone It is found in the stratosphere of atmosphere. It contains three atoms of oxygen (O_3). It is the poisonous form of oxygen.

The amount of CO_2 produced due to human activity such as burning of fossil fuels like coal, natural gas, petroleum, etc., and production of lime from limestone is much more than that consumed during photosynthesis. The consumption in photosynthesis has further decreased due to deforestation.

16. Volcanoes are called as natural source of air pollutant. Explain.

Ans. Volcanoes release large amounts of air pollutants such as carbon monoxide, sulphure dioxide, hydrogen sulphide, chlorine, hydrogen chloride, etc. Therefore, they are called as natural source of air pollutant.

17. (i) What is green house effect and what are its sources?

(ii) What is the role of CO_2 in the 'green house effect'?

(iii) Which rays cause greenhouse effect?

Ans. **(i)** Greenhouse effect is a naturally occurring phenomenon that is responsible for heating of Earth's surface and atomosphere due to the presence of certain gases in the atmosphere.

(ii) Heat from the sun after being absorbed by the earth is re-emitted by the earth and absorbed by CO_2 which then radiate it back to the earth, thus, maintaining the constant temperature of the earth.

(iii) Greenhouse gases absorb ultraviolet radiations and this results in greenhouse effect.

18. How are NO and NO_2 formed in the atmosphere?

Ans. NO is formed by the reaction of N_2 and O_2 during lightening or combustion of fossil fuels. It is further oxidised to NO_2.

19. (i) State any one difference between oxygen and ozone.

(ii) What is the reason behind the ozone layer getting depleted?

Ans. (i) Oxygen is diatomic (O_2), while ozone is triatomic (O_3).

(ii) Excessive use of man-made compounds containing both flourine and chlorine, e.g. CFCs, cause depletion of zone layer.

20. What would have happened if the green house gases were totally missing in the earth's atomosphere? Discuss.

Ans. Carbon dioxide, methane, water vapours, nitrous oxide, CFCs and ozone are green house gases. These gases trap some of the heat radiated by the earth's near the earth's surface and keep it warm.

This is called natural green house effect because it maintains the temperature and makes the earth perfect for life. If there were no green house gases, there would have been no vegetation and life on eath as the earth would be converted into a cold planet.

21. What are the ways of reducing greenhouse effect?

Ans. (i) Afforestation: Plant more trees.

(ii) Minimum use of automosibles: Use public transport.

(iii) Burning of fossil fuels should be minimised.

(iv) Deforestation should be stopped.

22. Explain how CFC breaks the ozone layer.

Ans. Chlorofluorocarbons are decomposed by ultra-violet rays to highly reactive chlorine, which is produced in its atomic form.

$$CF_2Cl_2(g) \xrightarrow{\text{Ultraviolet rays}} CF_2Cl(g) + \underbrace{Cl\ (g)}_{\text{Free radical}}$$

This free radical [Cl] reacts with ozone and chlorine monoxide is formed.

$$Cl(g) + O_3(g) \rightarrow ClO(g) + O_2(g)$$

This causes depletion of ozone, and chlorine monoxide further reacts with atomic oxygen to produce more free radicals of chlorine.

$$ClO(g) + O_3(g) \rightarrow Cl(g) + 2O_2$$

Again this free radical [Cl] destroys ozone, and the process continues, giving rise to large scale ozone, depletion.

23. Write some effects of global warming.

Ans. Some effects of global warming are:

(i) Due to global warming glaciers and polar ice cpas have started to melt and gradually this may lead to an increase in sea level.

(ii) Global warming will cause more water to evaporate from water bodies, thus forming more water vapour. Since water vapour also contributes to green house effect, global warming will further increase.

(iii) Global warming can lead to changes in rain patterns and thus shift in crop zones.

24. What do you understand by ppm?

Ans. Just as percent means out of a hundred. Thus, parts per million or ppm means out of a million. 1 ppm is equivalent to 1 milligram of something per litre of water or 1 milligram of something per kilogram soil.

25. (i) What is the effect of mercury compounds on leaving beings?

(ii) What are the harmful effects of oxides of sulphur?

Ans. (i) The inhalation of mercury vapour can produce harmful effects on the nervous digestive and immune system , lungs and kidneys.

(ii) It causes headache, vomiting and even death due to respiratory failure.

26. (i) Give an equation for the formation of ozone in the atmosphere. **[February, 2020]**

(ii) What is the function of ozone layer in the atmosphere?

(iii) Name a chemical which causes ozone depletion.

Ans. (i) Formation of ozone in atmosphere:

$$\underset{\text{Oxygen}}{O_2} \xrightarrow{\text{UV light}} O^{\infty} + O^{\propto}$$

$$O^{\infty} + O_2 \longrightarrow \underset{\text{Ozone}}{O_3}$$

Short Answer Type Questions

(ii) The function of the ozone layer is to shield the Earth from the harmful ultraviolet rays of the sun and to keep the Earth warm.

(iii) Chlorofluorocarbons cause ozone depletion. These release chlorine molecules in atmosphere which react with ozone and breakdown the ozone molecules, causing its depletion.

$$\underset{\text{Chlorine atom}}{Cl} + \underset{\text{ozone}}{O_3} \longrightarrow \underset{\text{chlorine monoxide}}{ClO} + \underset{\text{oxygen}}{O_2}$$

27. Oxidation of sulphur dioxide into sulphur trioxide in the absence of a catalyst is a slow process but this oxidation occurs easily in the atomosphere. Explain how does this happen. Give chemical reaction for the conversion of SO_2 into SO_3.

Ans. The presence of particulate matter in polluted air catalyses the oxidation of SO_2 to SO_3.
The oxidation of sulphur dioxide into sulphur trioxide can occur both photochemically or non-photochemically. In the ultraviolet region, the SO_2 molecules react with ozone photochemically.

$$SO_2 + O_3 \xrightarrow{bv} SO_3 + O_2$$

$$2SO_2 + O_2 \xrightarrow{bv} 2SO_3$$

Non-photochemically, SO_2 may be oxidised by moleculear oxygen in presence of dust and soot paticles.

$$2SO_2 + O_2 \xrightarrow{\text{Particulates}} 2SO_3$$

28. What do you mean by global warming? State the causes and effects of global warming.

Ans. The gradual and continous rise in average temperature of the Earth's surface is called **Global warming.**
Causes of Global Warming:

(i) High levels of gases, such as carbon dioxide (CO_2), methane (CH_4), ozone (O_3), nitrous oxide (NO), chlorofluorocarbons (CFCs) are responsible for blobal warming.

(ii) Burning of fossil fuels in homes and industies, deforesation, etc., increases the level of carbon dioxide and methane in atomosphere.

Effect of Global Warming:

(i) An increase in temperature would lead to melting of polar ice caps and consequent rise in sea levels.

(ii) Increase in temperature of Earth can cause change in weather and precipitation patterns on the Earth.

In the absence of greenhouse effect, the average temperature of Earth would have been 18°C rather than the present average temperature of 15°C Various sources are as follow:

(a) Oxides of Sulphur: These are produced when sulphur containing fossil fuel is burnt. SO_2 gas is poisonnous to both animals and plants.

(b) Oxides of Nitrogen: These are produced by the reaction of nitrogen and oxygen at high altitude when lightening strikes.

$$N_2(g) + O_2 \xrightarrow{1483K} 2NO(g)$$

$$2NO(g) + O_2(g) \longrightarrow 2NO_2(g)$$

$$NO(g) + O_3(g) \longrightarrow NO_2(g) + O_2(g)$$

(c) Hydrocarbons: Incomplete combustion of fuel used in atuomobiles is the major source for the release of hydrocabons. These are carcinogenic and cause cancer. They also harm plants.

(d) Oxides of Carbon: Carbon monoxide is one of the most serious air pollutants. It is highly poisonous to living beings because it blocks the supply of oxygen to the organs and tissues. It is produced due to the incomplete combustion of carbon. Carbon dioxide is the main contributor for global warming. It is released into the atmosphere by respiration, burning of fossil fuels and by decomposition of limestone during cement manufacturing.

29. What will happen, if:

(i) ozone gas is present in atmosphere?

(ii) all plants become extinct from the Earth?

Ans. (i) If ozone gas is present in atmosphere, then living organisms cannot survive because it is highly poisonous gas and harmful for living organisms.

(ii) We wll not be able to survive on Earth, if all plants become extinct because plants are the only source of oxygen in the atmosphere.

30. (i) What is the full form of CFC?

(ii) Give equation for the formation of ozone in the atmosphere.

(iii) What are the causes for the destruction of ozone layer?

Ans. (i) Chlorofluorocarbon.

(ii) $3O_2 \xrightarrow{\text{UV rays}} 2O_3$

(iii) The major causes for the destruction of ozone layer are:

(a) Excessive use of chlorofluorocarbon (b) Flying of supersonic planes.

31. Statues and monuments in India are affected by acid rain. How?

Ans. The air around the statues and monuments in India contains fairly high levels of oxides of sulphur and nitrogen. It is mainly due to a large number of industries and power plants around the areas. Oxides of nitrogen and sulphur are acidic in nature. SO_2 and NO_2 after oxidation and reaction with water are major contributors to acid rain.

$$2SO_2(g) + O_2(g) + 2H_2O(l) \longrightarrow 2H_2SO_4(aq)$$
$$4\,NO_2\,(g) + O_2\,(g) + 2H_2O(l) \longrightarrow 4HNO_3\,(aq)$$

This acid rain racts with marble of statues and monuments causing damage to these.

$$CaCO_3\,(s) + H_2SO_4\,(aq) \longrightarrow CaSO_4(s) + H_2O(l) + CO_2(g)$$

32. What are the adverse effect of nitrogen dioxide?

Ans. Nitrogen dioxide is a major atmospheric pollutant and adversely effects the human beings, plants and animals. The adverse effects of NO_2 are as follows:

(i) It causes irritation in mucous membrane.

(ii) Large quantities of NO_2 can lead to serious lung congestion and in same cases, can prove fatal.

(iii) The presence of nitrogen dioxide severely damages the leaves of the plants.

(iv) Nitrogen dioxide in the presence of light oxidises hydrocarbon leading to the formation of photochemical smong which cause irritation in eyes, asthma attack and other respiratory tract infections.

33. (i) List any four methods used to reduce formation of acid rain?

(ii) List any four methods that be used to reduce global warming?

Ans. (i) (a) By using less vehicles working on fossil fuels.

(b) By using catalytic converters in cars to reduce the effect of exhaust.

(c) By adding powdered limerstone to neutralise the acidic soil.

(d) By spreading information about the harmful effects of oxides of N and S.

(ii) The methods that can be used to reduce the global warming are as follows:

(a) Use of solar energy

(b) Afforestation

(c) Use of wet scrubbers

(d) Use of public transport

❑

Numericals

| Set 15 |

Chapter 1. Language of Chemistry

1. For the molecule $Na_2CO_3 . 10H_2O$ (washing soda), calculate the mas percentage of:
   (i) Water (ii) Sodium (Na) (iii) Carbon (C) (iv) Oxygen (O)

Ans.

$$\begin{aligned} \text{Molecular mass of } Na_2CO_3 . 10H_2O &= 2 \times 23 + 12 + 3 \times 16 + 10\,(2 + 16) \\ &= 46 + 12 + 48 + 180 \\ &= 286 \text{ amu} \end{aligned}$$

(i) In the molecule $Na_2CO_3.10H_2O$ mass of water is 180 g.
286 g of washing soda contains 180g of water

$$\begin{aligned} \text{100 g of washing soda contains} &= \frac{180}{286} \times 100 \\ &= 62.96\% \end{aligned}$$

Hence, mass percentage of water is 62.96 %.

(ii) In the molecule $Na_2CO_3.10H_2O$ mass of sodium is 46 g.
286 g of washing soda contains 46 g of sodium

$$\begin{aligned} \text{100 g of washing soda contains} &= \frac{46}{286} \times 100 \\ &= 16.08\ \% \end{aligned}$$

Hence, mass percentage of sodium is 16.08%.

(iii) In the molecule $Na_2CO_3.10H_2O$ mass of carbon is 12 g.
286 g of washing soda contains 12 g of carbon

$$\begin{aligned} \text{100 g of washing soda contains} &= \frac{12}{286} \times 100 \\ &= 4.19\% \end{aligned}$$

Hence, mass percentage of carbon is 4.19%.

(iv) In the molecule $Na_2CO_3.10H_2O$ mass of oxygen is 48 g
286 g of washing soda contains 48 g of oxygen

$$\begin{aligned} \text{100 g of washing soda contains} &= \frac{48}{286} \times 100 \\ &= 16.78\ \% \end{aligned}$$

Hence, percentage of oxygen is 16.78 %.

2. Calculate the relative molecular mass of the following:
   (i) $CHCl_3$ (ii) $(NH4)_2SO_4$ (iii) CH_3COONa (iv) $C_6H_{12}O_6$
   (v) $KClO_3$ (vi) $(NH4)_2Cr_2O_7$ (vii) $(NH_4)_2PtCl_6$

Ans.

(i) We have,

$$\begin{aligned} \text{Molecular mass of } CHCl_3 &= 12 + 1 + 3 \times 35.5 \\ &= 119.5 \text{ amu} \end{aligned}$$

(ii) We have, Molecular mass of $(NH_4)_2SO_4$ $= 2 \times 14 + 8 \times 1 + 32 + 16 \times 4$
$= 28 + 8 + 32 + 64$
$= 132$ amu

(iii) We have, Molecular mass of CH_3COONa $= 2 \times 12 + 3 \times 1 + 16 \times 2 + 35.5$
$= 24 + 3 + 32 + 35.5$
$= 94.5$ amu

(iv) We have, Molecular mass of $C_6H_{12}O_6$ $= 6 \times 12 + 12 \times 1 + 16 \times 6$
$= 72 + 12 + 96$
$= 180$ amu

(v) We have, Molecular mass of $KClO_3$ $= 39 + 35.5 + (16 \times 3)$
$= 39 + 35.5 + 48$
$= 122.5$ amu

(vi) As, Molecular mass of $(NH_4)_2\,Cr_2O_7$ $= (14 \times 2) + (1 \times 8) + (52 \times 2) + (16 \times 7)$
$= 28 + 8 + 104 + 112$
$= 252$ amu

(vii) As, Molecular mass of $(NH_4)_2\,PtCl_6$ $= (14 \times 2) + (1 \times 8) + 195.08 + (35.5 \times 6)$
$= 28 + 8 + 195.08 + 213$
$= 444.08$ amu

3. Calculate the percentage of carbon in carbon dioxide.

Ans. Atomic mass of carbon is 12 u and oxygen is 16 u.

We know, Molecular mass of CO_2 $= 12 + 16 \times 2$
$= 44$ u

44 g of CO_2 contains = 12 g carbon

100 g of CO_2 contains $= \frac{12}{44} \times 100 = 27.27$ g

Percentage of Carbon in CO_2 = 27.27 %

Hence, percentage of carbon is 27.27 %.

4. For the potassium chlorate $(KClO_3)$ molecule, calculate:

(i) Molecular mass
(ii) Mass percentage of Potassium (K)
(iii) Mass percentage of chlorine (Cl)
(iv) Mass percentage of Oxygen (O)

Ans.

(i) We know, Molecular mass of $KClO_3$ $= 39 + 35.5 + 3 \times 16$
$= 39 + 35.5 + 48$
$= 122.5$ amu

(ii) 122.5 g of potassium chlorate contains 39 g of potassium (K)

Therefore, 100 g of potassium chlorate contains potassium

$$= \frac{39}{122.5} \times 100$$

$= 31.84\%$

Hence, mass percentage of potassium is 31.84%.

(iii) 122.5 g of potassium chlorate contains 35.5 g of chlorine (Cl).

Therefore, 100 g of potassium chlorate contains:

$$= \frac{35.5}{122.5} \times 100$$

$= 28.98\%$

Hence, mass percentage of chlorine is 28.98%.

(iv) 122.5 g of potassium chlorate contains 48 g of oxygen (O).

Therefore, 100 g of potassium chlorate contains:

$$= \frac{48}{122.5} \times 100$$
$$= 39.18\%$$

Hence, mass percentage of oxygen is 39.18%.

5. Calculate the percentage mass of water in Epsom salt $MgSO_4.7H_2O$.

Ans. We have, Molecular mass of $MgSO_4.7H_2O$ = 24 + 32 + (16 × 4) + 7 (2 + 16)

= 24 + 32 + 64 + 126

= 246 amu

26 g of Epsom salt contains = 126 g of water of crystallisation

100 g of Epsom salt contains $= \frac{100 \times 126}{246}$

= 51.2 g

Therefore, perecentage of water in $MgSO_4.7H_2O$ is 51.2%.

6. The formula of a very important nitrogenous fertiliser is CON_2H_4. Calculate the percentage of carbon in this nitrogenous fertiliser. (C = 12, O = 16, N = 14 and H = 1)

Ans. We have,

Atomic mass of carbon is 12, oxygen is 16, nitrogen is 14 and hydrogen is 1.

Molecular mass of CON_2H_4 = 12 + 16 + (14 × 2) + (4 × 1)

= 12 + 16 + 28 + 4

= 60 amu

$$\text{Percentage of Carbon} = \frac{\text{Weight of Carbon}}{\text{Total weight of urea}} \times 100$$
$$= \frac{12}{60} \times 100$$
$$= 20\%$$

Therefore, percentage of C in CON_2H_4 is 20%.

7. Find the percentage of phosphorus for the following:

(i) $Ca(H_2PO_4)_2$

(ii) $Ca_3(PO_4)_2 = \frac{61.8}{233.8} \times 100$

Ans. (i) Molecular mass of $Ca(H_2PO_4)_2$ = 40 + (1 × 4) + (30.9 × 2) + (16 × 8)

= 40 + 4 + 61.8 + 128 = 233.8 g

233.8 g $Ca(H_2PO_4)_2$ contains = 61.8 g of phosphorous

100 g $Ca(H_2PO_4)_2$ contains $= \frac{61.8}{233.8} \times 100$

= 26.4 g

Therefore, percentage of Phosphorus is 26.4 %.

(ii) As, Molecular mass of $Ca_3(PO_4)_2$ = 3 × 40 + (30.9 × 2) + (16 × 8)

= 120 + 61.8 + 128 = 309.8 g

≈ 310 g

310 g $Ca_3(PO_4)_2$ contains = 61.8 g P

100 g $Ca_3(PO_4)_2$ contains $= \frac{100 \times 61.8}{310}$

= 19 g

Therefore, percentage of Phosphorus is 19%.

Numericals

8. (i) What is meant by relative molecular weight? **[November, 2019]**

(ii) Calculate the molecular weight of $Na_2CO_3.10H_2O$. **[November, 2019]**

[Na = 23; O = 16; C = 12; H = 1]

Ans. (i) Relative molecular mass: Relative molecular mass of a molecule is the average molecular mass of a substance when compared with 1/12 of the mass of an atom of Carbon-12.

$$\text{Relative molecular mass of a molecule} = \frac{\text{Average mass of one molecule of a substance}}{\text{Mass of 1/12 of an atom of Carbon-12}}$$

(ii) Molecular weight of $Na_2CO_3.10H_2O = 23 \times 2 + 12 + 16 \times 3 + 20 \times 1 + 10 \times 16$

$= 46 + 12 + 48 + 20 + 160$

$= 286$

9. (i) Calculate the molecular mass of ammonium carbonate $[(NH_4)_2CO_3]$. **[February, 2020]**

(ii) Find the percentage of nitrogen in urea $[NH_2CONH_2]$. **[February, 2020]**

[H = 1, C = 12, N = 14, O = 15]

Ans. (i) Molecular mass of ammonium carbonate can be calculated as follows:

$[(NH_4)_2CO_3]$

$N \times 2 + H \times 8 + C \times 1 + O \times 3 = 14 \times 2 + 1 \times 8 + 12 \times 1 + 16 \times 3$

$= 28 + 8 + 12 + 48$

$= 96$

So, molecular mass of ammonium carbonate is 96.

(ii) Molecular weight of Urea $[NH_2CONH_2]$ or N_2H_4CO:

$14 \times 2 + 1 \times 4 + 12 + 16 = 28 + 4 + 12 + 16 = 60$

$\% \text{ of N} = (28 / 60) \times 100$

$= 46.7\ \%$

Chapter 3. Water

1. 2 litre of acetone (liquid) is present in 80 litre of aqueous solution. Calculate its volume percent.

Ans. Given; Volume of solute = 2 litre

Volume of solution = 80 L

$$\text{Volume \%} = \frac{\text{Volume of solute}}{\text{Volume of solution}} \times 100$$

$$= \frac{2}{80} \times 100$$

$= 2.5\%$

2. 5 g of sodium hydroxide (solid) is present in 20 g solvent. Calculate mass percent.

Ans. Given, Mass of solute = 5 g

Mass of solvent = 20 g

Mass of solution = 20 + 5 = 25 g

$$\text{Mass \%} = \frac{\text{Mass of solute}}{\text{Mass of solvent}} \times 100$$

$$= \frac{5}{25} \times 100$$

$= 20\%$

3. Calculate the weight of sodium nitrate required for preparing a 60 g pure crystals from saturated solution of sodium nitrate solution at 70°C. Solubility of sodium nitrate is 140 g at 70°C and 100 g at 25°C.

Ans. Solubility at 70°C is 140 g and at 25°C is 100 g

Amount of crystals obtained when the solution is cooled from 70°C to 25°C.

$= 140 - 100$

$= 40$ g

To obtain 40 g of crystals, sodium nitrate taken is 140 g.

Therefore, to obtain 60 g crystal, sodium nitrate required

$$= \frac{140}{40} \times 60$$
$$= 210 \text{ g}$$

Therefore, required weight of sodium nitrate is 210 g.

4. To make a 100 mL of solution, 30 mL of alcohol is mixed with 70 mL of water. Calculate volume percent of the solution.

Ans. Given, Volume of solute is 30 mL.

Volume of solvent is 70 mL.

$$\text{Volume percent} = \frac{\text{Volume of solute}}{\text{Volume of solvent + Volume of solute}} \times 100$$
$$= \frac{30}{30+70} \times 100$$
$$= \frac{30}{100} \times 100 = 30\%$$
$$= 30\ \%$$

Hence, the volume percent 30%.

5. Hydrate calcium sulphate has the formula of $CaSO_4.2H_2O$. **[February, 2020]**

(i) What is the name given to the water molecules present in the salt?

(ii) Calculate the percentage of water molecules in hydrated calcium sulphate.

[Ca = 40; S = 32; O – 16; II = 1]

Ans. (i) In $CaSO_4.2H_2O$, the water molecules attached are known as water of crystallisation, which is the fixed number of water molecules chemically attached to each formula unit of a salt in its crystalline form.

(ii) Molecular weight of hydrated calcium sulphate = $CaSO_4.2H_2O$

$Ca \times 1 + S \times 1 + O \times 4 + (H_2O) \times 2 = 40 + 32 + 64 + 36 = 172$

Now in 172 g, 36 g is water.

Hence, $(36/172) \times 100 \approx 21\ \%$

Percentage of water is 21%.

6. What will be the mass percentage of solute if 50 g sugar is dissolved in 450 g of water?

Ans. Given, Mass of solute is 50 g

Mass of solvent is 450 g

Therefore,

$$\text{Mass percent} = \frac{\text{Mass of solute}}{\text{Mass of solvent + Mass of solute}} \square 100$$
$$= \frac{50}{50+450} \times 100$$
$$= \frac{30}{500} \times 100 = 6\%$$

Hence, the mass percent is 6%

7. For making a saturated solution, 136 g of salt is dissolved in 500 g of water at 293 K. Calculate its solubility at this temperature.

Ans. As we know, 500 g of water dissolves = 136 g of salt

$$100 \text{ g of water dissolves} = \frac{136 \times 100}{500} = 27.2 \text{ g}$$

Therefore, solubility is 27.2 g.

8. In a sodium chloride solution, 15 g of sodium chloride is dissolved in 285 g of water. Calculate the concentration of the solution.

Ans. Given, Mass of solute = 15 g

Numericals

Mass of solvent = 285 g

Mass of solution = 285 + 15 = 300 g

Therefore,

$$\text{Mass \%} = \frac{\text{Mass of solute}}{\text{Mass of solvent}} \square 100$$

$$= \frac{15}{300} \times 100$$

$$= 5\%$$

Therefore, concentration of the solution is 5%.

9. If 4 litres of an organic compound is present in 90 litres of an aqueous solution. Calculate its volume percent.

Ans. Given, Volume of solute = 4 litre

Volume of solution = 90 litre

Therefore,

$$\text{Volume\%} = \frac{\text{Volum of solute}}{\text{Volum of solution}} \square 100$$

$$= \frac{4}{90} \times 100 = 4.44\%$$

Thus, volume percent is 4.44%

10. Find the solubility of potassium chloride when 12 g of saturated solution of potassium chloride at 20°C is evaporated to dryness and leaves a solid residue of 3 g.

Ans. Weight of water = 12 g – 3g = 9 g

$$\text{9 g of water dissolves} = \text{3 g of solid}$$

$$\text{100 g of water dissolves} = \frac{3 \times 100}{9}$$

$$= 33.3 \text{ g}$$

Therefore, solubility KCl is 33.3 g.

11. Calculate the solubility of potassium nitrate at 20°C if the mass of empty dish is 50 g, mass of dish and solution is 65 g, and mass of dish and residue is 54.3 g.

Ans. Given, Mass of empty dish = 50 g

Mass of dish and solution is = 65 g

Mass of solution = 65 g – 50 g = 15 g

So, Mass of dish and residence is = 54.3 g

$\Rightarrow$ Mass of residue = 54.3 g – 50 g

= 4.3 g

Mass of solvent = 15 g – 4.3 g

$\Rightarrow$ = 10.7 g

10.7 g of water dissolves = 4.3 g of solid

$$\Rightarrow \quad \text{100 g of water dissolves} = \frac{4.3 \times 100}{10.7}$$

Hence , solubility of potassium nitrate is 40.18 g

12. What will be the concentration of the solution if 20 g of KCl is dissolved in 400 g of water?

Ans. Given, Mass of solute is 20 g

Mass of solvent is 400 g

Therefore,

$$\text{Mass percent} = \frac{\text{Mass of solute}}{\left(\begin{array}{c}\text{Mass of solvent +} \\ \text{Mass of solute}\end{array}\right)} \times 100$$

$$= \frac{20}{(20 + 400)} \times 100$$

$$= \frac{20}{420} \times 100$$

$$= 4.76\%$$

13. What will be the concentration at 293 K, if 36 g of NaCl is dissolved in 100 g of water at this temperature?

Ans. Given, Mass of solute is 36 g
Mass of solvent is 100 g

Therefore,

$$\text{Mass percent} = \frac{\text{Mass of solute}}{\text{Mass of solvent + Mass of solute}} \square 100$$
$$= \frac{36}{36+100} \times 100$$
$$= \frac{36}{136} \times 100$$
$$= 26.47\ \%$$

Hence, concentration is 26.47.

14. Can the following groups of elements be classfied as Dobereiner's triad? Explain by giving reason.

(i) Na, Si, Cl (ii) Be, Mg, Ca

(Atomic mass of Be 9; Na 23; Mg 24; Si 28; Cl 35; Ca 40)

Ans. (i) No, because Si has an average atomic mass than that of Na and Cl. But they do not resemble in their properties. Na (23); Si (28); Cl (35)

$$\text{Atomic mass of Si} = \frac{23+35}{2} = \frac{58}{2} = 29$$

(ii) Yes, Be (9); Mg (24); Ca (40)

$$\text{Atomic mass of Mg} = \frac{9+40}{2} = \frac{49}{2} = 24.5$$

It can be classified as Dobereiner's triads because the middle element of the triad had both atomic mass and properties similar to average of the two other elements of the triad.

Chapter 7. Study of Gas Laws

1. To what temperature must a gas at 300 K be cooled down in order to reduce its volume to 1/3rd of its original volume if the pressure remains constant?

Ans. Initial temperature (T_1) is 300 K, initial volume is V_1 and final volume is $\frac{1}{3}V_1$, we have to calculate the final temperature, that is, T_2.

From Charles' law,

$$\left(\text{As, } V_2 = \frac{V_1}{3}\right)$$
$$\frac{V_1}{300} = \frac{V_1}{3\,T_2}$$
$$T_2 = 100\text{ K}$$

Hence, the final temperature is 100 K.

2. Prove that the volume of a gas at 273°C is twice its volume at 273 K at constant temperature.

Ans. Let the volume of gas at 273°C (T_1) be V_1 and volume of gas at 273 K (V_2) is V_2.

From Charles' law,

$$\frac{V_1}{T_1} = \frac{V_2}{T_2}$$

$$\Rightarrow \quad \frac{V_1}{546} = \frac{V_2}{273}$$

$$\Rightarrow \quad V_1 = \frac{546}{273}V_2$$

$$\Rightarrow \quad V_1 = 2V_2$$

So, volume of gas at 273°C is twice than the volume of gas at 273 K.

3. 16 g of oxygen gas is enclosed in 1dm^3 flask at 25°C. Calculate the pressure exerted by the gas, if the molecular mass of any gas occupies 22.4 litres at S.T.P.

Ans. Oxygen (O_2) molecule is a diatomic molecule. Molecule mass of O_2 is 16 × 2 = 32 g.
So, 32 g of oxygen occupies 22.4 dm^3 at S.T.P.

$$16 \text{ g of oxygen will occupy} = \frac{22.4\,dm^3}{32} \times 16$$

$$= 11.2\ dm^3$$

Thus,
$P_1 = 1$ atm, $P_2 = ?$
$V_2 = 11.2\ dm^3$ $V_2 = 1\ dm^3$
$T_1 = 273$ K, $T_2 = 273 + 25 = 298$ K
From ideal gas equation,

$$\frac{P_1V_1}{T_1} = \frac{P_2V_2}{T_2}$$

$$\Rightarrow \quad P_2 = \frac{P_1V_1T_2}{T_1V_2}$$

$$\Rightarrow \quad = \frac{1 \times 11.2 \times 298}{273 \times 1}$$

$$\Rightarrow \quad = 12.2 \text{ atm}$$

So, the pressure exerted by the gas is 12.2 atm.

4. 50 cm^3 of hydrogen gas is collected over water at 17°C and 750 mm Hg pressure. Calculate the volume at STP of a dry gas. The vapour pressure of the dry gas at 17°C is 14 mm Hg.

Ans. Volume of a dry gas at STP is:

V = 50 cm^3, $V_1 = ?$
P = 750 – 14 = 736 mm, $P_1 = 760$ mm
T = 290 K, $T_1 = 273$ K

According to the ideal gas law equation,

$$\frac{PV}{T} = \frac{P_1V_1}{T_1}$$

$$\Rightarrow \quad \frac{736 \times 50}{290} = \frac{760 \times V_1}{273}$$

$$\Rightarrow \quad V_1 = 45.6\ cm^3$$

5. What would be the necessary temperature for the volume of a gas to be doubled initially at STP if the pressure is decreased to 25%.

Ans. Temperature for the volume of a gas to be doubled initially at STP if the pressure is decreased to 25%is:
$V_1 = V$, $V_2 = 2$ V
$P_1 = 760$ atm, $P_2 = \frac{25}{100} \times 760 = 190$ mm of Hg
$T_1 = 273$ K, $T_2 = ?$
According to the gas equation:

$$\frac{P_1V_1}{T_1} = \frac{P_2V_2}{T_2}$$

$$\Rightarrow \quad \frac{760 \times V}{273} = \frac{190 \times 2V}{T_2}$$

$$\Rightarrow \quad T_2 = \frac{190 \times 2 \times 273}{760}$$

$$\Rightarrow \quad T_2 = 136.5 \text{ K}$$

6. A cylinder having a capacity of 20 liters contains at 100 atm pressure. How many flask of 200 cm^3 capacity can be filled from it at 1 atm pressure, temperature remaining constant.

Ans. Given information is as follows:

$P = 100$ atm, $P_1 = 1$ atm
$V = 20$ L, $V_1 = ?$
$T = T_1$,
Using gas equation to calculate the volume;

$$\frac{PV}{T} = \frac{P_1V_1}{T_1}$$

$$\Rightarrow \quad \frac{100\times 20}{T} = \frac{1\times V_1}{T}$$

As, $V_1 = 2000$ litres $= 2\ m^3$ (1000 litres $= 1\ m^3$)

$$\Rightarrow \quad \text{Volume of one flask} = \frac{200}{100\times 100\times 100} m^3$$

$$\Rightarrow \quad \text{Number of flasks} = \frac{2\times 1000000}{200} = 10000$$

$$\Rightarrow \quad \text{Number of flasks} = 10000$$

7. 561 dm^3 of gas at STP condition is filled in a container having 748 dm^3 capacity. Calculate the percent change required in pressure at constant temperature.

Ans. Initial volume of gas = 561 dm^3
Final volume of gas = 748 dm^3
Difference in volume = 748 – 561 = 187 dm^3
At constant temperature, decrease in the pressure percentage:

$$\frac{187}{748}\times 100 = 25\%$$

Hence, the decrease in the pressure percentage is 25%.

8. What would be the required temperature for the volume of a gas to be doubled initially at STP if the pressure is decreased to:
(i) 25% (ii) 50%

Ans. Temperature for the volume of a gas to be doubled initially at STP if the pressure is
(i) Decreased to 25%
$V_1 = V$, $V_2 = 2\ V$
$P_1 = 760$ atm, $P_2 = \frac{25}{100}\times 760 = 190$ mm of Hg
$T_1 = 273K$, $T_2 = ?$
According to the gas law equation,

$$\frac{P_1V_1}{T_1} = \frac{P_2V_2}{T_2}$$

$$\Rightarrow \quad \frac{760\times V}{273} = \frac{190\times 2V}{T_2}$$

$$\Rightarrow \quad T_2 = \frac{190\times 2\times 273}{760}$$

$$\Rightarrow \quad T_2 = 236.5K$$

(ii) Decreased to 50%
$V_1 = V$, $V_2 = 2\ V$
$P_1 = 760$ atm, $P_2 = \frac{50}{100}\times 760 = 380$ mm of Hg
$T_1 = 273$ K, $T_2 = ?$
According to the gas law equation,

$$\frac{P_1V_1}{T_1} = \frac{P_2V_2}{T_2}$$

$\Rightarrow \quad \frac{760 \times V}{273} = \frac{380 \times 2V}{T_2}$

$\Rightarrow \quad T_2 = 273\ K$

9. Calculate the minimum pressure required to compress 500 dm^3 of air at 1 bar to 200 dm^3, if temperature remains constant.

Ans. Given, $V_1 = 5\,00\ dm^3$ $V_2 = 200\ dm^3$
$P_1 = 1$ bar, $P_2 = ?$

From Boyle's law,

$$P_1V_1 = P_2V_2$$

$\Rightarrow \quad 500 \times 1 = P_2 \times 200$

$\Rightarrow \quad P_2 = \frac{500}{200}$

$\Rightarrow \quad = 2.5$ bar

10. 130 cm^3 of a gas is taken at 27.3 K. The temperature is then raised to 0°C answer the following:
(i) What is the new volume of the gas at the same reaction condition at constant pressure?
(ii) What will be the new volume when the initial volume is reduced to 100 cm^3 at constant pressure?

Ans. (i) We have, $V_1 = 130\ cm^3$, $T_1 = 27.3\ K$
$V_2 = ?$ $T_2 = 273\ K$ (since 0°C = 273 K)

By Charles' law,

$$\frac{V_1}{T_1} = \frac{V_2}{T_2}$$

Substituting the values,

$\Rightarrow \quad \frac{130}{27.3} = \frac{V_2}{273}$

$\Rightarrow \quad V_2 = \frac{130 \times 273}{27.3}$

$\Rightarrow \quad V_2 = 1300\ cm^3$

The new volume of the gas at 0°C will be 1300 cm^3.

(ii) We have, $V_1 = 100\ cm^3$, $T_1 = 27.3\ K$
$V_2 = ?\ cm^3$, $T_2 = 273\ K$ (since 0°C = 273 K)

By Charles' law,

$\Rightarrow \quad \frac{V_1}{T_1} = \frac{V_2}{T_2}$

Substituting the values, $\frac{100}{27.3} = \frac{V_2}{273}$

$\Rightarrow \quad V_2 = \frac{100 \times 273}{27.3}$

$\Rightarrow \quad V_2 = 1000\ cm^3$

The new volume of the gas at 0°C will be 1000 cm^3.

11. Determine the temperature of a gas enclosed in cylinder under S.T.P. when ($1/6^{th}$) of its initial volume, pressure remaining constant.

Ans. Let the initial volume be V_1 and Final volume will be $\frac{V_1}{6}$
Given, Initial temperature $T_1 = 273\ K$
Final temperature $T_2 = ?$
According to Charles's law,

$$\frac{V_1}{T_1} = \frac{V_2}{T_2}$$

Substitute the given values in the above equation, we get

$\Rightarrow \quad \frac{V_1}{273} = \frac{V_1/6}{T_2}$

$\Rightarrow \quad T_2 = \dfrac{V_1 \times 273}{6 \times V_1} = \dfrac{273}{6} = 45.5 \text{ K} = 45.4 - 273 = -227.5\text{YC}$

Hence, the temperature at which the volume of enclosed gas is 1/6 th of its initial volume is –227.5°C.

12. Determine the temperature of a gas enclosed in cylinder under S.T.P. when half of its initial volume, pressure remaining constant.

Ans. Let the initial volume be V_1 and Final volume will be $\dfrac{V_1}{2}$

Initial temperature $T_1 = 273$ K

Final temperature T_2=?

According to Charles' law, $\dfrac{V_1}{T_1} = \dfrac{V_2}{T_2}$

Substitute the given values in the above equation, we get

$\Rightarrow \quad \dfrac{V_1}{273} = \dfrac{V_1/2}{T_2}$

$\Rightarrow \quad T_2 = \dfrac{V_1 \times 273}{2 \times V_1} = \dfrac{273}{2} = 136.5\text{K} = 136.5 - 273 = -136.5\text{YC}$

Hence, the temperature at which the volume of enclosed gas is ($1/2^{th}$) of its initial volume is –136.5°C.

13. 22.4 L of a gas weighs 70 g at STP condition. Calculate the weight of the gas if the gas occupies 20 L and 700 mm Hg of pressure.

Ans. We have,

$V_1 = 20$ L, $\quad V_2$ =?

$P_1 = 700$ mm Hg, $\quad P_2 = 760$ mm Hg

$T_1 = 300$ K, $\quad T_2$= 273 K

Using the gas law equation; $\dfrac{P_1V_1}{T_1} = \dfrac{P_2V_2}{T_2}$

$\Rightarrow \quad \dfrac{700 \times 20}{300} = \dfrac{760 \times V_2}{273}$

$\Rightarrow \quad V_2 = \dfrac{91 \times 7}{76} = \dfrac{637}{38} = 16.76 \text{ L}$

22.4 L of the gas at STP weighs = 70 g

16.76 L of the gas has weight at STP = $\dfrac{70 \times 16.76}{22.4} = 52.38\text{g}$

14. LPG cylinder having a pressure of 14.9 atm. The pressure of the gauge of the cylinder shows 12 atm pressure at 27°C. At what temperature will the cylinder explode?

Ans. Given, $P_1 = 14.9$ atm, $P_2 = 12$ atm

$V_1 = 28 \text{ cm}^3$, $V_1 = V_2$

T_1 =?, $T_2 = 300$ K

Using the gas law equation,

$\dfrac{P_1V_1}{T_1} = \dfrac{P_2V_2}{T_2}$

$\Rightarrow \quad \dfrac{14.9 \times V_1}{T_1} = \dfrac{12 \times V_1}{300}$

$\Rightarrow \quad T_1 = 372.5 \text{ K}$

$\Rightarrow \quad T_1 = 372.5 \text{ K} - 273 = 99.5°\text{C}$

Hence, the temperature when cylinder will explode is 99.5°C

15. Determine the volume of the dry air at STP condition that occupies 28 cm^3 at 14°C and 750 mm Hg pressure when saturated with water vapour. The vapour pressure of the water at 14°C is 12 mm Hg.

Ans. Pressure due to dry air is P_1 and P_2.

We have, $P_1 = 750 - 12 = 738$ mm Hg, $P_2 = 760$ mm Hg

$T_1 = 14°C = 14 + 273 = 287$ K, $T_2 = 0°C = 273$ K

$V_1 = 28\ cm^3$, V_2=?

Using the gas law equation,

$$\frac{P_1V_1}{T_1} = \frac{P_2V_2}{T_2}$$

$$\Rightarrow \quad \frac{738 \times 28}{287} = \frac{760 \times V_2}{273}$$

$$\Rightarrow \quad V_2 = 25.9\ cm^3$$

Hence, volume of dry air at STP is 25.9 cm^3.

16. A carbon dioxide sample occupies 30 cm^3 at 15°C and 740 mm of pressure. Determine its volume at STP conditions.

Ans. We have, $P_1 = 740$ mm Hg, $P_2 = 760$ mmHg

$T_1 = 288$ K, $T_2 = 273$ K

$V_1 = 30\ cm^3$, V_2 =?

Using the gas law equation,

$$\frac{P_1V_1}{T_1} = \frac{P_2V_2}{T_2}$$

$$\Rightarrow \quad \frac{750 \times 30}{288} = \frac{760 \times V_2}{273}$$

$$\Rightarrow \quad V_2 = 27.7 cm^3$$

Hence, volume occupied by carbon dioxide at STP is 27.7 cm^3.

17. Determine the final volume of a gas 'Y' if the original pressure of this given gas is doubled and its temperature is increased three times.

Ans. We have, $P_1 = 1$ atm, $P_2 = 2$ atm

$T_1 = T$, $T_2 = 3$ T

$V_1 = Y$, V_2 =?

Using the gas law equation,

$$\frac{P_1V_1}{T_1} = \frac{P_2V_2}{T_2}$$

$$\Rightarrow \quad \frac{1 \times Y}{T} = \frac{2 \times V_2}{3T}$$

$$\Rightarrow \quad V_2 = \frac{1 \times Y \times 3T}{T \times 2} = \frac{3}{2}Y = 1\frac{1}{2}Y$$

Thus, the final volume is $1\frac{1}{2}$ times the original volume.

18. A gas occupies 3 L at 0°C. Determine the volume of this gas at –20°C temperature at constant pressure.

Ans. We have, $P_1 = P_2 = P$,

$T_1 = 0°C = 0 + 273 = 273K$, $T_2 = -20°C = -20 + 273 = 253$ K

$V_1 = 3$ L, V_2 =?

Using the gas law equation,

$$\frac{P_1V_1}{T_1} = \frac{P_2V_2}{T_2}$$

$$\Rightarrow \quad \frac{P \times 3}{273} = \frac{P \times V_2}{253}$$

$$\Rightarrow \quad V_2 = \frac{3 \times 253}{273} = 2.78 L$$

Thus, volume occupied by gas at –20°C and contant messure is 2.78l.

19. Determine the minimum pressure required to compress 500 dm^3 of air at 1 bar to 200 dm^3 at constant temperature.

Ans. We have, $V_1 = 500\ cm^3$, $V_2 = 500\ cm^3$
$T_1 = 273\ K$, $T_2 = 273\ K$
$P_1 = 1$ bar, P_2 =?
Using the gas law equation,

$$\frac{P_1V_1}{T_1} = \frac{P_2V_2}{T_2}$$

$$\Rightarrow \quad \frac{1\times 500}{273} = \frac{P_2\times 500}{273}$$

$$\Rightarrow \quad P_2 = \frac{P_2\times 500}{273} = 2.5\ \text{bar}$$

Thus, minimum pressure required to compress 500 dm^3 of air is 2.5 bar.

20. Convert the following:
(i) 273° C to Kelvin (ii) 293 K to °C

Ans. (i) 273°C in Kelvin
t°C = tK – 273
273°C = tK – 273
tK = 273 + 273 = 546 K
∴ 273°C = 546 K

(ii) 293 K in °C
t°C = tK – 273
t°C = 293 – 273
t°C = 20°C
∴ 293 K = 20°C.

21. At constant temperature, a gas is at a pressure of 540 mm of mercury. At what pressure its volume decreases by 60%.

Ans. Let the initial volume of gas $(V_1) = x$
∴ 60% of initial volum e $= \frac{60}{100}x = 0.6x$

∴ The final volume of gas $(V_2) = x - 0.6x = 0.4x$
The initial pressure of gas (P_1) = 540 mm Hg
Final pressure of gas (P_2) =?
Using Boyle's law, $P_1V_1 = P_2V_2$

$$\Rightarrow \quad P_2 = \frac{P_1V_1}{V_2} = \frac{540\times x}{0.4x} = 1350\ \text{mm Hg}$$

22. If the volume of certain gas was found 400 cm^3, when pressure was 520 mm of Hg. What would be the new volume of the gas if the pressure is increased by 30%?

Ans. Given, Initial volume of gas, $V_1 = 400\ cm^3$
Initial pressure of ga, P_1 = 520 mm Hg
30% of initial pressure $= 520 \times \frac{30}{100} = 156$ mm Hg

23. Calculate the pressure of 2.5 litre of dry hydrogen gas, if it occupies as volume of 3 litres at 1.2 atmosphere and constant temperature.

Ans. Here, P_1 =?, V_1 = 2.5 litres, P_2 = 1.2 atm, V_2 = 3.0 litres

Now, using Boyle's law, $P_1V_1 = P_2V_2$

$$\Rightarrow \quad P_1 \times 2.5 = 1.2 \times 3.0$$

$$\Rightarrow \quad P_1 = \frac{1.2\times 3.0}{2.5} = 1.44\ \text{atm}$$

24. A gas occupies the initial volume of 400 cm^3 at a pressure Z. If the pressure is changed to 5 atmosphere, the volume of the gas was found to be 200 cm^3. Calculate the value of Z.

Ans. Given, $P_1 = Z$, $P_2 = 5$ atm, $V_1 = 400\ cm^3$, $V_2 = 200\ cm^3$
Using Boyle's law, $P_1V_1 = P_2V_2$

$$\Rightarrow \quad Z \times 400 = 5 \times 200$$

$$\Rightarrow \quad Z = \frac{5\times200}{400} = 2.5 \text{ atm}$$

25. At constant temperature a gas occupies a volume of 2000 cm^3 at a pressure of 740 mm of mercury. Find at what pressure its volume will be 500 cm^3.

Ans. Initial volume of the gas, $V_1 = 2000\ cm^3$
Initial pressure of the gas, $P_1 = 740$ mm Hg
Final volume of the gas, $V_2 = 500\ cm^3$
Final pressure of the gas, $P_2 = ?$
∴ According to Boyle's law, $P_1V_1 = P_2V_2$

$$\Rightarrow \quad 740 \times 2000 = P_2 \times 500$$

$$\Rightarrow \quad P_2 = \frac{2000\times740}{500} = 2960 \text{ mm Hg}$$

26. (i) Express 775 K in Celsius scale. **[November, 2019]**
(ii) The volume of given mass of a gas in a container is 100 ml at 760 mm Hg pressure. Calculate the pressure at which the gas would occupy a volume of 80 ml, temperature remaining contant. **[November, 2019]**

Ans. (i) We know that:

$$T_{(°C)} = T_{(K)} - 273.15$$

Hence,

$$T_{(°C)} = 775 - 273.15$$
$$= 501.85\ °C$$

(ii) Initial Volume = 100 mL; Pressure = 760 mm Hg; Final Volume = 80 mL; Temperature remains constant.
We know that:

$$P_iV_i = P_fV_f \text{ (Temperature is constant)}$$
$$760 \times 100 = P_f \times 80$$
$$P_f = 760 \times \frac{100}{80}$$
$$= 950 \text{ mm Hg}$$

Hence, the gas would occupy a volume of 80 mL at 950 mm Hg.

27. A fixed volume of a gas occupies 228 cm^3 at 27°C and 70cm of mercury what is its volume at STP? **[February, 2020]**

Ans. We know that $P_1V_1/T_1 = P_2V_2/T_2$
At STP, temperature is 273 K and pressure is 1 atm.
Given,

$$P_1 = 70 \text{ cm of Hg} = 0.92105 \text{ atm (1 atm = 76 cm Hg)}$$
$$V_1 = 0.228 \text{ L}$$
$$T_1 = 300 \text{ K}$$
$$P_2 = 1 \text{ atm}$$
$$T_2 = 273 \text{ K}$$

$$\frac{(0.92105 \text{ atm} \times 0.228 \text{ L})}{300 \text{ K}} = \frac{(1 \text{ atm} \times V_2)}{273 \text{ K}}$$

$$V_2 = 0.19 \text{ L or } 190\ cm^3$$

www.ingramcontent.com/pod-product-compliance
Ingram Content Group UK Ltd.
Pitfield, Milton Keynes, MK11 3LW, UK
UKHW061704190726
13853UKWH00008B/2395

9 789392 563881